MAKE IT Mystery

An anthology of short mystery plays

CRAIG SODARO

Meriwether Publishing Ltd., Publisher
PO Box 7710
Colorado Springs, CO 80933-7710

Editor: Arthur Zapel
Assistant Editor: Audrey Scheck
Cover design: Jan Melvin

Library of Congress Cataloging-in-Publication Data

Sodaro, Craig.
  Make it mystery : an anthology of short mystery plays / by Craig Sodaro.
    p. cm.
  ISBN-13: 978-1-56608-115-3 (pbk.)
  ISBN-10: 1-56608-115-7 (pbk.)
1. Detective and mystery plays, American. 2. Young adult drama, American.
3. One-act plays, American. I. Title.
PS625.5S67 2006
812'.052708--dc22

                              2006011856

1   2   3   06   07   08

Dedication

To my girls — Sue, Sally, Amy, Katie, and Betsy.

Contents

Introduction

Who doesn't like a mystery?

The recipe is classic: A crime committed during a blinding snowstorm ... a group of tantalizing suspects each with motive, opportunity, and means ... a wary sleuth ... clues littering the landscape ... escalating danger as the truth begins to surface ... the final scene when the sleuth reveals the criminal and the irrefutable evidence that serves up justice.

Agatha Christie knew the recipe well. Her classic play, *The Mousetrap,* is the longest-running play in history, still delighting audiences after fifty-four years, even though by now everyone knows that _____ did it! What a testament to the appeal of a stage mystery!

The most important ingredient in a mystery is a secret — one kept from most of the characters and definitely from the audience. The characters and the audience thus become partners in discovering the secret, and if the audience can outguess the characters, all the better!

Make It Mystery's menu includes twelve one-act plays with something to suit every taste and age group. For young performers, *Mystery of the Magical Forest* and *Mommy's a Zombie!* are mysteries laced with plenty of comedy. For middle school performers, *The Mother Goose Mystery, Clue in the Library,* and *Case of the Dangerfield Diamond* provide enjoyable characters seasoned with lots of buried secrets.

Queen of Hearts is a nice side dish to a study of Shakespeare, who plays the role of detective before he earns fame as a playwright. In *The Mermaid* and *For Better or Worse,* women must somehow find the courage to outwit adversaries who threaten their happiness — and lives. Classic mystery entrees include *A Very Cold Case, Into Thin Heir,* and *The Little Women Mystery,* designed for an all-female cast. For dessert, *Where Did Everybody Go?* whips up a mystery spiced with a bit of the supernatural.

Whatever your choice from the menu, *bon appetit!*

— Craig Sodaro

1

Queen of Hearts

Synopsis:
William Shakespeare disappeared from his hometown of Stratford when he was eighteen. No one knows why he left his wife and children, though historians have a number of theories. One tells of Will poaching a deer on Sir Thomas Lucy's land — a serious offense that could have seen Will in jail or executed. How he made his way to London and got started in theatre is also a mystery. *Queen of Hearts* takes an imaginative look at what might have happened to young Will Shakespeare.

Characters (5 male, 6 female):
WILL SHAKESPEARE, a young playwright
MRS. DOGBERRY, mistress of the Boar's Head Inn
MR. DOGBERRY, her husband
BESS, a waitress at the Inn
ANGELA, another waitress
ANNIE DULL, an older woman
SIR THOMAS LUCY, a distinguished guest at the Inn
LADY LUCY, his wife
MR. GREENE, another guest
MAGISTRATE
MRS. BURBAGE

Setting:
The Boar's Head Inn in London, spring of 1588. Wing entrance Down Right leads to outside. Wing entrance Down Left leads to upstairs and other rooms at the Inn. Fireplace Up Center. Tables and benches here and there. Bar or high table Up Left.

Props:
Cloths/rags; deck of playing cards; broom; feather quill, ink, and papers for Will; coins; purse or small bag for money; satchel for Greene; bread and butter on plate; jam jar; drinking glasses or mugs; several old boxes; envelope.

Costumes:
Long dresses for all female characters or skirts and blouses. Aprons for Anna, Bess, and Mrs. Dogberry along with mop hats if available. Long-sleeve, blousy shirts for Mr. Dogberry, Will, and Magistrate along with dark pants rolled up to knees with long, white stockings. Vests can also be worn. Add a jacket for Lucy and perhaps a cape for Greene. An "old man" disguise is needed for Will. This includes a beard, hat with long white hair attached, and a long cloak or cape covering his other costume.

1
2
3   (*AT RISE: WILL sits at table Upstage writing in a*
4   *frustrated manner. BESS and ANGELA wipe table*
5   *tops. MRS. DOGBERRY stands at bar playing cards*
6   *with ANNIE DULL. MR. DOGBERRY sweeps the floor*
7   *lazily.*)
8 MRS. DOGBERRY: You missed a whole pile of dirt
9   over there, Mr. Dogberry!
10 MR. DOGBERRY: Maybe you'd like to do the sweeping
11   for a change, Mrs. Dogberry!
12 MRS. DOGBERRY: Don't you go gettin' sassy with me!
13   Do the job right, hear?
14 ANNIE: So, now, what am I supposed to do with these
15   cards?
16 MRS. DOGBERRY: If you have a two of hearts or
17   diamonds or spades, you can put your two down.
18   If you have a five of hearts, you can put that down
19   because it's a wild card.
20 ANNIE: Oh, dear, these new-fangled games!
21 BESS: Nothin' new about playing cards.
22 ANGELA: 'Ceptin' those are from France, all fancy-like.
23 MRS. DOGBERRY: (*Proudly*) Only the best for me, girls.
24   And when you own an inn like the Boar's Head,
25   you can buy the best, too!
26 MR. DOGBERRY: 'Tis me that owns the Boar's Head,
27   Mrs. Dogberry!
28 MRS. DOGBERRY: (*Sweetly*) But what's yours is mine,
29   my dear! Well, Annie, what're you waitin' for?
30 ANNIE: All right! I'll put these down! (*ANNIE lays two*
31   *cards down.*)
32 MRS. DOGERRY: A pair of twos. Now ain't that
33   convenient! (*MRS. DOGBERRY turns over another*
34   *card from a pile on the bar.*) Well, now, a queen of
35   hearts.

1   BESS: Heard the hearts are bad luck!
2   ANGELA: Aye! Turn one of 'em over 'n you're a goner.
3   MRS. DOGBERRY: You've been listenin' to too many
4   old wives' tales. I win, Annie, my dear! I win!
5   *(MRS. DOGBERRY moves to WILL.)* **And speakin' of**
6   tales, how's your old wives' tale coming, Mr.
7   Shakespeare? *(No response as WILL scribbles)* **Mr.**
8   Shakespeare? I say, the man is deaf!
9   BESS: Shhh! He's concentrating.
10 ANGELA: Writing his play!
11 ANNIE: Writing a what?
12 BESS: A play for the theatre.
13 ANGELA: There's very good money in it.
14 BESS: The playhouses are always full.
15 ANGELA: And the acting companies are always busy!
16 ANNIE: But what's he writing about?
17 WILL: About people who are very, very quiet.
18 MRS. DOGBERRY: See here! If you want quiet, go up
19   to that room I've been rentin' you for a pittance.
20 WILL: It's too hot up there. The ink runs.
21 MRS. DOGBERRY: As if your ink has anything to say.
22 MR. DOGBERRY: Leave the gent alone, Madam! He's
23   a paying guest.
24 MRS. DOGBERRY: Is he, Mr. Dogberry? How many
25   weeks of rent do you owe now, Mr. Shakespeare?
26 WILL: I'll have your money as soon as I've finished my
27   play.
28 MRS. DOGBERRY: And who's to buy this thing?
29 WILL: Well, I'm sure Pembroke's Men or Lord
30   Strange's Men ... or even Lord Chamberlain's Men
31   will pay dearly for a comedy about a shrew who
32   can't find a husband.
33 MR. DOGBERRY: A shrew! Now isn't that a
34   coincidence!
35 MRS. DOGBERRY: You go and haul that garbage out

1   of here, Mr. Dogberry, before I take a broom to
2   you! *(She turns from MR. DOGBERRY, who sticks his*
3   *tongue out at her as he exits Right.)* **And as for you,**
4   **Master Shakespeare, Mr. Theatricality Extraordinaire**
5   **... unless I get my sixpence for back rent by**
6   **tomorrow, you'll find yourself scribbling outside in**
7   **the gutter.**
8   BESS: Oh, Mrs. Dogberry, you can't be so cruel!
9   ANGELA: Mr. Shakespeare is sure to be a wonderful
10   success!
11   MRS. DOGBERRY: Then you two can go join him in
12   his success! Bar maids are easier to find than
13   grains of soot in London, and that's a fact. Get
14   back to work! *(BESS and ANGELA do so; WILL*
15   *returns to his writing.)* **And now, Annie, dear, a**
16   **wager. A shilling if I can guess a card you pull at**
17   **random from the deck. What say you? You're a**
18   **gambler, aren't you?**
19   ANNIE: I pull a card from the deck, and you tell me
20   which one it is?
21   BESS: Doesn't sound possible, if you ask me.
22   ANNIE: Not in the least! You're on, Mrs. Dogberry!
23   MRS. DOGBERRY: There you go ... pull a card. Now
24   don't let me see it, but show it to Bess there.
25   *(ANNIE does so.)* **You've seen it, Bess?**
26   BESS: Aye.
27   MRS. DOGBERRY: Now, slip your card on the top of
28   the deck here. *(ANNIE does so. MRS. DOGBERRY*
29   *quickly shuffles the deck.)* **I'll place the top ten cards**
30   **face up on the table.** *(She does so.)* **Any of 'em**
31   **yours, Annie?**
32   ANNIE: *(Proudly)* **Nope! And I'll thank you for my**
33   shilling now.
34   MRS. DOGBERRY: But this one is! *(MRS. DOGBERRY*
35   *pulls card from the bottom of the deck and lays it on*

1   *the bar.)* **That the card, Bess?**

2 **BESS: Aye!**

3 **ANNIE: You're a witch! How could you —**

4 **MRS. DOGBERRY: A shilling, if you don't mind, Annie!**

5 **ANNIE:** *(Tossing a coin on bar)* **That's the work of the**

6   **devil, I say!** *(ANNIE exits Right as MRS. DOGBERRY*

7   *laughs heartily.)*

8 **WILL: Not worth giving credit even to the devil. All**

9   **you did was slip Annie's card to the bottom of the**

10   **deck and then made it look like you were shuffling**

11   **the cards. After you laid out the ten cards, you just**

12   **pulled the bottom card from the deck and, of**

13   **course, it was Annie's card.**

14   *(BESS and ANGELA laugh.)*

15 **MRS. DOGBERRY:** *(Proudly)* **Still, that trick got me a**

16   **shilling. More than any of you'll earn in a day!**

17   *(SIR THOMAS LUCY and LADY LUCY enter Right.)*

18   **Oh, my, now look at this!**

19 **THOMAS: I say, Madam, are you mistress of this**

20   **establishment?**

21 **MRS. DOGBERRY: And a finer establishment you'll**

22   **not find in all London!**

23   *(WILL sneaks Off Right without being seen by the*

24   *LUCYs.)*

25 **LADY: It's not a fine establishment at all, but it suits**

26   **my husband's tight purse strings.**

27 **THOMAS: Say no more, Lady Lucy, or we shall not be**

28   **visiting your sister tomorrow.**

29 **MRS. DOGBERRY:** *(Impressed)* **Lady! Well, my, and you**

30   **must be Sir Thomas Lucy from Stratford.**

31 **THOMAS: The same. Have you any accommodations?**

32 **MRS. DOGBERRY: The finest!**

33 **LADY: Ha!**

34 **THOMAS: You must forgive my wife. She aspires to the**

35   **palace itself.**

1   LADY: Where we could have stayed, but for my
2   husband's desire not to be indebted to anyone.
3   THOMAS: Neither a borrower nor a lender be!
4   MRS. DOGBERRY: Why, you sound like Master
5   Shakespeare.
6   THOMAS: *(Angrily)* William Shakespeare?
7   MRS. DOGBERRY: Why he's sitting right — *(MRS.*
8   *DOGBERRY looks where WILL was sitting, but finds*
9   *him gone.)*
10 THOMAS: William Shakespeare from Stratford?
11 MRS. DOGBERRY: The same! A very prominent
12   playwright, I'll have you know. But come along,
13   and I'll show you our finest suite. In fact, good
14   Queen Bess herself once stayed here while the
15   palace was under repairs. *(MRS. DOGBERRY leads*
16   *THOMAS and LADY Off Left.)*
17 BESS: *(Sarcastically)* Good Queen Bess herself!
18 ANGELA: That woman lies like a rug!
19 BESS: But Sir Lucy did have a fine line, Master
20   Shakespeare —
21 ANGELA: He's gone! Left all his papers and all.
22 BESS: We've got to write that line down for him.
23 ANGELA: About Good Queen Bess?
24 BESS: *(Writing)* "Neither a borrower nor a lender be."
25   Will can probably do something with that.
26 ANGELA: Ha! I gave him that one, "To be or not to
27   be," and all he said was "That is the question."
28   *(MR. GREENE enters Right.)*
29 MR. GREENE: Good day to you!
30 BESS: Good day, sir.
31 MR. GREENE: The name's Greene. Robert Greene.
32 ANGELA: Would you like a pint, sir?
33 MR. GREENE: Later. First, a room.
34 BESS: Well, now, Mr. Greene, our mistress is upstairs
35   with another party, but she'll be glad to help you

9

1   as soon as she comes down.
2   MR. GREENE: *(Holding up a purse)* I've got more than
3   enough money to pay. *(MRS. DOGBERRY enters*
4   *Left.)* Gold, see here? *(He pulls coins from purse.)*
5   Payment for my play, "Friar Bacon."
6   BESS: Blimey, Mr. Greene! That's a lot of money! You
7   ought not flash it about like that.
8   ANGELA: Mighty tempting to thieves.
9   MRS. DOGBERRY: *(Haughtily)* There are no thieves at
10   the Boar's Head, Mr. Greene. Your person and
11   effects are completely secure within these spotlessly
12   clean walls.
13 ANGELA: Mr. Greene's a playwright, too.
14 MR. GREENE: There's another here?
15 BESS: Master William Shakespeare! And what he can't
16   do with a turn of words!
17 MRS. GREENE: Never heard of the lad.
18 MRS. DOGBERRY: Because he's a worthless piece of
19   baggage who can't pay his bills on time, sir. I am
20   Mrs. Dogberry, proprietress of these premises.
21   *(MR. DOGBERRY enters Left.)* You're needing a
22   room, I understand?
23 MR. GREENE: That I do.
24 MRS. DOGBERRY: We've a fine room overlooking the
25   bridge and right next to Sir Thomas Lucy and his
26   wife.
27 MR. GREENE: Good as royalty, that is! I wonder if
28   he's interested in becoming a patron.
29 ANGELA: He's a bit on the stingy side.
30 BESS: Wouldn't open his purse for St. Peter himself.
31 MRS. DOGBERRY: You two get about your business!
32   And if you'll follow me, Mr. Greene ... and do tell,
33   where is your play being performed?
34 MR. GREENE: At the Rose.
35 MRS. DOGBERRY: Mr. Dogberry, make a point of

1 reminding me so I may take in the play next week
2 **Wednesday.** *(MRS. DOGBERRY exits Left, followed*
3 *by MR. GREENE.)*
4 **MR. DOGBERRY: Anything to get you out of the house,**
5 **my dear!**
6 *(WILL enters Right, cautiously.)*
7 **WILL: Pssst! Bess! Angela!**
8 **BESS: Master Shakespeare! You disappeared mighty**
9 **quick.**
10 **WILL: Aye! And I need your help.**
11 **ANGELA: What's wrong?**
12 **WILL: Go up to my room ... and there by the bed you'll**
13 **find a box full of costumes. Bring it to me in the**
14 **alley next door.**
15 **BESS: The alley?**
16 **WILL: Aye! And don't ask any more questions!**
17 *(BESS and ANGELA race Off Left. WILL looks at*
18 *DOGBERRY, who smiles.)*
19 **MR. DOGBERRY: My lips are sealed!**
20 *(The curtain falls.)*
21
22 <center>Scene Two</center>
23
24 *The following morning.*
25 *(AT RISE: BESS and ANGELA clean the room.*
26 *ANNIE sits at the table eating bread. MRS.*
27 *DOGBERRY sits with ANNIE buttering her bread.)*
28 **MRS. DOGBERRY: Dogberry! Where are you with that**
29 **jam?**
30 *(MR. DOGBERRY saunters in carrying a jar of jam.)*
31 **MR. DOGBERRY: Here you are, Mrs. Dogberry.**
32 **MRS. DOGBERRY: About time!** *(MR. DOGBERRY moves*
33 *behind bar and washes or dries glasses.)*
34 **ANNIE: Nice of you to treat me to breakfast.**
35 **MR. DOGBERRY: Oh, there's no treat here, Annie. She**

11

1   wants something, that's for sure!
2   MRS. DOGBERRY: Go on and get!
3   *(MR. GREENE races on Left.)*
4   MR. GREENE: I've been robbed!
5   MRS. DOGBERRY: Mr. Greene! Please, sit down!
6   Relax, and tell me about it in a very quiet voice.
7   MR. GREENE: *(Shouting)* Somebody came in and took
8   my purse! All my money's gone!
9   *(THOMAS and LUCY enter Left.)*
10   THOMAS: What's all the commotion?
11   MR. DOGBERRY: Moneybags here got robbed.
12   BESS: Told you you shouldn't have flashed that gold
13   around like that!
14   MR. GREENE: I'll do as I please! That doesn't give
15   anybody the right to steal my money!
16   MRS. DOGBERRY: I'll just go upstairs and have a look
17   around. *(Suspiciously)* We haven't seen Mr.
18   Shakespeare yet today, have we? Perhaps he
19   knows something. *(MRS. DOGBERRY exits Left.)*
20   ANNIE: I'll fetch the magistrate!
21   MR. GREENE: Who's this Shakespeare fellow?
22   ANGELA: We told you ... a playwright.
23   BESS: He writes the noblest words.
24   THOMAS: In fact, sir, he's a thief and scoundrel!
25   LADY: Oh, Thomas, stop it.
26   THOMAS: He is!
27   LADY: Just because he shot one of your precious deer.
28   THOMAS: The man was poaching!
29   LADY: He had a wife and two children to feed!
30   MR. GREENE: So he's a wanted man!
31   BESS: That's impossible to believe!
32   ANGELA: He doesn't seem like a criminal at all.
33   *(WILL, disguised now as an old man, enters Right and*
34   *sits at table near Right entrance.)*
35   THOMAS: I tell you, the best of these rascals don't

1 seem any different than you and I! Their true
2 nature only comes out when the sun goes down
3 and the moon comes up.
4 BESS: You're scarin' me!
5 WILL: Pardon me, sir, but are you an authority on
6 criminal ways?
7 LADY: You needn't take everything he says on face
8 value, Master —
9 WILL: Master ... Master ... Falstaff.
10 MR. GREENE: Do you know this Shakespeare fellow,
11 Master Falstaff?
12 WILL: Oh, indeed! In fact, I came this morning to
13 discuss one of his plays with him.
14 ANGELA: But we've not seen him since last night.
15 THOMAS: Any idea where he might have gone, old
16 man?
17 WILL: Could be right under our noses ... or more
18 likely Hampton Heath. He likes a stroll up there
19 to clear his mind.
20 THOMAS: And perhaps poach off somebody else's
21 land. I'll put my money on Shakespeare as the
22 thief!
23 WILL: Could be, but you'll never catch him.
24 MR. GREENE: Oh? And why not?
25 WILL: He's slippery as an eel. Too full of confidence
26 and talent. There's too much he's got to do yet in
27 his life to be interrupted by gettin' hanged at
28 Tyburn!
29 *(MAGISTRATE enters Right with ANNIE.)*
30 MAGISTRATE: All right, now! What's this I hear?
31 Somebody's been robbed?
32 MR. GREENE: I have, Magistrate!
33 MAGISTRATE: What'd the thief take?
34 MR. GREENE: Five gold coins.
35 MAGISTRATE: A considerable amount of money.

1   MR. GREENE: And my purse!

2   *(MRS. DOGBERRY enters Left holding purse.)*

3   MRS. DOGBERRY: Your purse has been recovered!

4   *(She holds it up.)*

5   MAGISTRATE: Is that it?

6   MR. GREENE: *(Snatching it away)* It is!

7   MRS. DOGBERRY: Sadly, it's empty.

8   THOMAS: Where did you find the purse, Mrs.

9   Dogberry?

10   MRS. DOGBERRY: *(With great satisfaction)* Mr.

11   Shakespeare's room, where else?

12   BESS: Blimey!

13   ANGELA: I can't believe it!

14   MAGISTRATE: Who's this Shakespeare?

15   WILL: An up-and-coming playwright. Hangs about

16   Hampton Heath, I hear.

17   MAGISTRATE: Oh, one of them theatre people. Well,

18   they all come to no good, and this proves it.

19   MRS. DOGBERRY: Stealin's the only way they can put

20   up their playhouses.

21   MAGISTRATE: The devil's work!

22   THOMAS: What are you going to do about it?

23   MAGISTRATE: You said Hampton Heath, old man?

24   THOMAS: I'll go along with you! I'll know him on

25   sight! And there's a further offense —

26   LADY: You are going nowhere, Thomas, but to my

27   sister's. This is no concern of yours.

28   THOMAS: Madam! If I can catch this scoundrel now,

29   he'll pay dearly for his crime years ago.

30   LADY: *(Firmly)* My sister is waiting for us, and we shall

31   not be late. Is that clear?

32   THOMAS: *(To MAGISTRATE)* Let me know the moment

33   you catch the rascal!

34   MAGISTRATE: I shall, sir.

35   LADY: Come along, Thomas. I believe our carriage is outside.

1 THOMAS: I tell you, Shakespeare will hang if I have
2   anything to say about it! *(THOMAS and LADY exit*
3   *Right.)*
4 WILL: *(Under his breath)* Good thing you won't!
5 MAGISTRATE: What was that, sir?
6 WILL: I said, "God thinks you're right."
7 MR. GREENE: Magistrate, I'll accompany you to the
8   Heath, for he might be dangerous!
9 MAGISTRATE: Then come along. *(To MR. DOGBERRY)*
10   We'll be back when we've found something. And,
11   Dogberry, if he returns here, hold him!
12 MR. DOGBERRY: How'll I hold a thief?
13 MRS. DOGBERRY: Don't you worry. I got an iron pot
14   that'll crack his skull!
15   *(MAGISTRATE and MR. GREENE exit Right.)*
16 WILL: Such a shame. And I did so want to discuss his
17   play this morning.
18 MRS. DOGBERRY: What could you do for him? You're
19   just a poor old beggar who'd better have enough
20   money to pay for his bread!
21 WILL: I've enough, Madam. In fact, I've enough to
22   wager in a small game of cards.
23 MRS. DOGBERRY: *(Brightening)* Cards?
24 WILL: I can see a pack in your apron, there. Your
25   mistress enjoys games, doesn't she, girls?
26 BESS: Why, yes, sir!
27 ANGELA: But she always wins.
28   *(WILL whispers to BESS and ANGELA under next*
29   *lines.)*
30 ANNIE: Well, now, Mrs. Dogberry, the gentleman
31   seems eager to lose what little money he has.
32 MRS. DOGBERRY: *(Pulling out her cards)* Aye! I just
33   wonder what game this stranger's up to! *(BESS*
34   *and ANGELA exit Left.)* You sure you want to do
35   this, Master Falstaff?

1 WILL: It's just a pleasant diversion.
2 MR. DOGBERRY: Well, it's your funeral!
3 *(The curtain falls.)*
4
5 **Scene Three**
6
7 *That afternoon.*
8 *(AT RISE: MRS. DOGBERRY stands behind bar.*
9 *WILL, still dressed as old man, sits at table. ANGELA*
10 *and BESS enter Left carrying several boxes.)*
11 BESS: This is the last of his things.
12 ANGELA: We'll sure miss him!
13 MRS. DOGBERRY: What, that thief? The least he could
14 have done when he stole that money from Mr.
15 Greene was to pay me what he owed me!
16 *(MAGISTRATE, MR. GREENE, and THOMAS enter*
17 *Right.)* What news? Have you found the wretch?
18 MAGISTRATE: Not a sign of him anywhere!
19 MR. GREENE: I just came to get my things, and then
20 I'm on my way, never to stay here again! *(MR.*
21 *GREENE exits Left, MRS. DOGBERRY trying to*
22 *follow.)*
23 MRS. DOGBERRY: Well, you can't blame it on the
24 Boar's Head!
25 THOMAS: Mrs. Dogberry, I managed to leave my wife
26 at her sister's but felt finding Shakespeare of too
27 much importance to let the thing go.
28 MAGISTRATE: But we've turned up nothing.
29 THOMAS: So here is the address of my wife's sister
30 where you can reach me should this man show up.
31 *(He hands MRS. DOGBERRY an envelope. MRS.*
32 *BURBAGE enters Right. She sits at table. BESS waits*
33 *on her during next dialog.)*
34 MRS. DOGBERRY: Why, I shall be more than happy to
35 keep my eyes and ears open.

1   WILL: I'm sure you'll eventually catch the rascal. After
2   all, he's a fine playwright.
3   MRS. DOGBERRY: Bah!
4   MAGISTRATE: What would you know about it, old
5   man?
6   WILL: Not much, but if his plays do end up getting
7   presented at one of the playhouses—
8   ANGELA: And they surely will, sir!
9   MRS. DOGBERRY: You shut your mouth, insolent
10   creature!
11   WILL: When they end up being presented, he should
12   be easy enough to find.
13   THOMAS: True, but the likelihood of that happening is
14   the same as lightning striking me dead this
15   instant! *(WILL quickly looks up as if waiting for the*
16   *lightning.)*
17   MAGISTRATE: He'll probably sink into the gutter
18   somewhere like the thieving rat he is and take his
19   chances running.
20   WILL: *(To MRS. DOGBERRY)* Speaking of chances,
21   Madam ... perhaps I could show you a card trick?
22   MRS. DOGBERRY: What? Haven't you lost enough to
23   me already today?
24   WILL: But we've got an audience!
25   MRS. DOGBERRY: Well, now ... have you still something
26   to wager?
27   WILL: A shilling left, Madam.
28   MRS. DOGBERRY: So be it! And what is this wager?
29   WILL: I wager I can make a card fly over to Angela,
30   there, without anyone seeing it!
31   MAGISTRATE: *(Laughing)* What? That's ridiculous!
32   THOMAS: Sounds like witchcraft to me!
33   WILL: Come, come! Merely slight of hand!
34   MRS. DOGBERRY: You're a mighty big fool for a man
35   your age.

1   WILL: Anyone else care to lay a wager?

2   MAGISTRATE: I'll wager a shilling that you can't do

3   such a thing!

4   THOMAS: And I!

5   MRS. DOGBERRY: I'll wager two!

6   WILL: The cards, Mrs. Dogberry? The ones we played

7   with earlier will be fine. *(MRS. DOGBERRY hands*

8   *WILL the deck of cards from her apron.)* And is this

9   a full deck?

10 MRS. DOGBERRY: Of course it's a full deck!

11 WILL: Every card accounted for?

12 MRS. DOGBERRY: You can take my word for it!

13   *(WILL spreads the cards on the table and fans them out*

14   *face down. He pulls out one card.)*

15 WILL: The three of hearts. *(He pulls another card.)* The

16   king of clubs. *(And another)* The ace of diamonds.

17   Yes, seems like they're all here. But to make one

18   fly to Angela, I'll have to utter that magic Arabian

19   word, abracadabra! Now, count the cards, Sir

20   Lucy.

21 THOMAS: *(Counting)* One, two, three ... ten ... twenty

22   one ... thirty-three ... thirty-eight ... forty-five ...

23   fifty ... fifty-one.

24 MAGISTRATE: Fifty-one?

25 BESS: But a deck must have fifty-two.

26 MRS. DOGBERRY: You must have counted wrong!

27 THOMAS: I certainly did not! *(As MRS. DOGBERRY*

28   *counts again)* There are fifty-one cards there! One

29   is missing!

30 MRS. DOGBERRY: This is ridiculous! We'll just turn

31   them over! *(She does so with the help of THOMAS and*

32   *MAGISTRATE.)*

33 MAGISTRATE: Which one's missing?

34 THOMAS: A face card! The queen of hearts!

35 WILL: Angela, what card do you hold in your apron?

1   ANGELA: *(Pulling card from apron pocket)* **The queen of**
2   **hearts!**
3   MRS. DOGBERRY: How'd you get that?
4   ANGELA: It belongs with the deck. You can see it is
5   the same picture as the other queens.
6   MAGISTRATE: So it is!
7   THOMAS: How did you do that, sir? It's quite a trick!
8   WILL: It was no trick at all.
9   MRS. DOGBERRY: It is! No one touches these cards
10   but me! They're always in my apron! *(She angrily*
11   *gathers the cards.)*
12 WILL: All except the queen of hearts, which you
13   dropped last evening.
14 MRS. DOGBERRY: Dropped where?
15 WILL: In Mr. Greene's room when you stole his money!
16 MAGISTRATE: What?
17 MRS.   DOGBERRY: That's   ridiculous!   William
18   Shakespeare stole that money! I found Mr.
19   Greene's purse in Shakespeare's room!
20 WILL: You only said you did. You actually kept the
21   purse for that very reason.
22 BESS: We found the card in Mr. Greene's room.
23 MRS. DOGBERRY: Then I ... I must have dropped it
24   earlier!
25 ANGELA: We found it after he said he'd been robbed.
26 WILL: And you had the queen of hearts just before
27   that when you were playing a game with Annie
28   Dull.
29 MRS. DOGBERRY: Surely you don't believe any of
30   this!
31 THOMAS: I really must be on my way. Good day, all!
32   *(WILL blocks THOMAS's departure.)*
33 WILL: Going so soon, Sir Lucy?
34 THOMAS: Yes, my wife awaits me at her sister's estate.
35 WILL: But you owe me a shilling! *(Angrily THOMAS*

1   *pulls out a shilling and hands it to WILL.)*
2   THOMAS: Now let me pass! *(MR. DOGBERRY enters*
3   *Left.)*
4   MR. DOGBERRY: Now, will you look at this! A
5   handkerchief holding five gold pieces!
6   MRS. DOGBERRY: Where'd you get those?
7   MR. DOGBERRY: Under our mattress, Mrs. Dogberry!
8   In your little treasure box!
9   MAGISTRATE: That's quite a treasure!
10   MRS. DOGBERRY: I told you never to touch my
11   things!
12   THOMAS: Let me pass, I say!
13   MRS. DOGBERRY: *(Pointing to THOMAS)* He's the one
14   who put me up to it! Gave me ten shillings to put
15   the robbery on William Shakespeare so he'd rot in
16   jail!
17   THOMAS: This is ridiculous! I never did such a thing!
18   MAGISTRATE: *(To MRS. DOGBERRY)* You admit you
19   stole Mr. Greene's money?
20   MRS. DOGBERRY: Only on his say-so! *(THOMAS*
21   *pushes past WILL and races Off Right.)*
22   WILL: I don't suppose Master Shakespeare will have to
23   worry about him any longer.
24   MAGISTRATE: *(Indicating MRS. DOGBERRY)* Nor this
25   one! Come along with me!
26   MRS. DOGBERRY: What about Sir Lucy?
27   MAGISTRATE: He's a knight of the realm! Such an
28   accusation as this won't go very far! *(MAGISTRATE*
29   *pulls MRS. DOGBERRY Right.)*
30   MRS. DOGBERRY: Mr. Dogberry! Help me! You can't
31   leave me to rot in Tyburn! *(MAGISTRATE exits with*
32   *MRS. DOGBERRY in hand.)*
33   BESS: Aren't you going to help her, Mr. Dogberry?
34   ANGELA: I'm sure you can buy a light sentence.
35   MR. DOGBERRY: I'll help her, all right. But not 'til

1 tomorrow. I've been waiting a long time for a
2 night of peace and quiet. *(MR. GREENE enters Left,*
3 *carrying a bag.)* Oh, Mr. Greene, your gold has been
4 found. *(He hands GREENE the coins.)*
5 MR. GREENE: I thank you, Mr. Dogberry! But if I ever
6 see that Shakespeare fellow again — *(MR.*
7 *GREENE crosses Right.)*
8 BESS: But, Mr. Greene, it wasn't Mr. Shakespeare at
9 all!
10 MR. GREENE: At least I know a thief will never make
11 a name for himself in the theatre! *(He exits Right.)*
12 ANGELA: But, Mr. Greene! You don't understand!
13 WILL: *(As himself now)* Let him go, Angela. He wouldn't
14 listen anyway. *(WILL removes his disguise.)*
15 MR. DOGBERRY: Master Shakespeare? You've been
16 right here all along?
17 WILL: With the help of some friends.
18 BESS: We couldn't let Mr. Shakespeare run off.
19 ANGELA: How would he ever finish his play?
20 WILL: I'm afraid, though ... I might never make
21 anything of myself if people are so quick to want
22 my demise!
23 *(MRS. BURBAGE rises and moves to WILL.)*
24 MRS. BURBAGE: There's a critic born every minute.
25 WILL: I fear you're right, Madam.
26 MRS. BURBAGE: That was quite a performance. I'm
27 glad I stopped in for a scone and had a chance to
28 see you.
29 WILL: We all perform well if our lives depend on it.
30 MRS. BURBAGE: My husband heads up a troupe of
31 actors. He lost one of his men to a family situation
32 and needs a replacement. Would you be
33 interested?
34 WILL: Aye, Madam! I would be most interested!
35 BESS: And Mr. Shakespeare writes plays, too!

1 ANGELA: The most wonderful adventures.
2 MRS. BURBAGE: What are your plays about, Mr.
3   Shakespeare?
4 WILL: I have just finished one about the reign of
5   Henry the Sixth ... and I am working on another
6   about a shrew who learns to hold her tongue.
7 MRS. BURBAGE: Then you write from experience.
8   Stay here and I shall send my husband presently.
9 WILL: Thank you, Madam! But I don't even know your
10   name.
11 MRS. BURBAGE: Mrs. Burbage. Mrs. James Burbage.
12   *(She exits Right.)*
13 WILL: James Burbage! He's head of the Earl of
14   Leicester's Men! He owns a theatre!
15 DOGBERRY: Well, my boy, there's hope for you, after
16   all! *(He slaps WILL on the back as the curtain falls.)*

Clue in the Library

Synopsis:
An old library in jeopardy from a demolition team ... whispers of a hidden treasure ... a body found in the stacks ... and dedicated teens who just might be able to save the day.

Characters (4 male, 7 female):
SAUL SLAUGHTER, a private eye
MS. GRUNDY, a librarian
ALICE, a high school student
EMILY, a high school student
KAITLIN, a high school student
MS. PINCHFORK, a developer
CORNELIUS CRUMP, a caretaker
MONICA HARVEY, a realtor
EUNICE DAVENPORT, a homemaker who always wears a hat
ALISTER BANKS, a businessman
DETECTIVE FORTUNE

Setting:
The Carterville Town Library. Wing entrance Right leads to outside; wing entrance Left leads to other areas of the library. Librarian desk Right. Empty bookshelves Upstage here and there. A dusty table Left set with two or three overturned or broken chairs. A crooked picture of Cornelius Carter hangs Up Center. Beneath portrait is a fireplace complete with mantel. Edges of bookcase Left are decorated with a series of dots, numbers, and hyphens.
Note: The characters on the bookcase can be accurately portrayed as in the script — a series of numbers (negative and positive) separated by dots. The design, however, can be somewhat fancy and antiqued so that the audience can't really see the exact information.
Note: To make the lift-top on the mantel, just cut a board the size of the existing mantel, attach with hinges along the wall side, and add an edge that hangs slightly over the existing mantel so that the audience won't notice the extra board on top.

Props:
Key; notepad and pencil; purses for women; several working flashlights; small pistol; cellphones; pad of paper and pencil; length of rope; mop; envelope containing a small piece of well-worn paper.

Costumes:
Modern, everyday dress for all characters.

Sound Effects:
Gunshot, thunder

1	<div align="center">**Scene One**</div>
2	*Late one night.*
3	*(AT RISE: The stage is dimly lit. SAUL SLAUGHTER*
4	*enters Right pocketing a key. He holds notepad and*
5	*pencil. He looks around the room.)*
6	**SAUL:** *(To himself, nervously)* **Spooky old place. No**
7	**wonder they want to tear it down ... not even a**
8	**terminal for a computer!** *(Looking at portrait)* **Well,**
9	**Old Man Carter, this library of yours is about to**
10	**join you in the great beyond. But not until I find**
11	**your treasure. Everybody knows it's here, but I'm**
12	**going to be the one to find it ... and when I do ...**
13	**my client's going to be so pleased. Of course, I'll**
14	**take most of the cash off the top for expenses ... a**
15	**businessman like you would understand that! And**
16	**my client will never know the difference, right?**
17	*(Looking at bookcase Left)* **Well, well, well ... what**
18	**have we here? I think this might be just what**
19	**we're looking for! My ticket to easy street!** *(A shot*
20	*rings out. SAUL falls, as does the curtain.)*
21	
22	<div align="center">**Scene Two**</div>
23	
24	*Sidewalk in front of the library, played before the curtain.*
25	*(AT RISE: MS. GRUNDY enters Left, followed by*
26	*ALICE, EMILY, KAITLIN, MONICA, ALISTER,*
27	*EUNICE, and MS. PINCHFORK.)*
28	**MS. GRUNDY:** *(As a tour guide, pointing into the audience)*
29	**You can see the influence of Frank Lloyd Wright**
30	**in the exterior design of the library.**
31	**MONICA: Who?**
32	**ALICE: You know, the great architect?**
33	**EMILY: See the prairie design just above the gutters?**
34	**MS. PINCHFORK: Those are dead leaves!**
35	**EUNICE: Why hasn't anyone cleaned them out?**

25

1 MS. GRUNDY: Cornelius, our handyman, can only do
2   so much.
3 KAITLIN: *(Quickly)* A group of us from the high school
4   are going to take care of it this weekend.
5 ALISTER: If that's any indication of what shape this
6   building's in, it should come down, Frank Floyd
7   Bright or not.
8 MS. GRUNDY: But then there'd be no library in
9   Carterville.
10 ALICE: What's a town without a library?
11 MS. PINCHFORK: With the Internet, who needs a
12   library?
13 ALISTER: We need to move into the twenty-first
14   century!
15 MS. GRUNDY: With another mall?
16 MS. PINCHFORK: Strip malls are all the rage, Ms.
17   Grundy.
18 EUNICE: I buy all my hats at strip malls. And I think
19   this is a perfect location for one. I live right
20   around the corner!
21 MS. PINCHFORK: You can walk to the mall! No traffic
22   jams! No looking for a parking space!
23 ALICE: Can I ask you a question, Ms. Davenport?
24   How did you get to be on the town-planning
25   commission?
26 EUNICE: Well, I saw an ad in the paper for a hat sale
27   right above the little notice about volunteers
28   needed for the planning commission, and I dialed
29   the planning commission by mistake, and, well,
30   here I am!
31 MS. GRUNDY: Please, let's go into the library and
32   you'll get a feel for how sturdy and well-
33   constructed the building is.
34 MONICA: Actually, I've seen enough.
35 ALISTER: And I've got to meet a client in ten minutes.

1 EMILY: But you have to come inside!
2 MS. PINCHFORK: But you're wasting the commissioner's
3   time!
4 MS. GRUNDY: But you're not voting until tomorrow's
5   meeting.
6 ALICE: And the Save the Library Committee has worked
7   very hard on our presentation.
8 KAITLIN: You'll be amazed by what you see!
9   *(MS. GRUNDY leads ALL except ALICE, EMILY and*
10   *KAITLIN Off Right, grumbling.)*
11 ALICE: I hope they're amazed.
12 KAITLIN: Listen, if we can get even one of them to
13   vote against the strip mall, we'll get our service
14   learning credit.
15 EMILY: Is a grade all you can think about, Kaitlin?
16 KAITLIN: *(Coyly)* That's not all I think about.
17 ALICE: Yeah ... there's always Jeff. And Bob ... and
18   Tom.
19 KAITLIN: *(Laughing)* **Jealous?** *(EMILY exits Right*
20   *followed by ALICE and KAITLIN as lights dim.)*
21
22   **Scene Three**
23
24 *The library interior, immediately after.*
25   *(AT RISE: SAUL's body still lies on the floor, but in*
26   *the dim light, no one can see him — yet. MRS.*
27   *GRUNDY enters Right, followed by MONICA,*
28   *ALISTER, MS. PINCHFORK, EUNICE, ALICE,*
29   *KAITLIN, and EMILY.)*
30 MS. GRUNDY: *(Proudly)* **Here we are, folks! The main**
31   **room, built in 1922, remodeled in 1965. As you can**
32   **see, it has a spacious atmosphere.**
33 MONICA: I can't see a thing!
34 ALISTER: Aren't there any lights?
35 EMILY: Right over here! *(EMILY flips light switch, but*

1   *nothing happens.)*
2   ALICE: I guess the electricity's turned off.
3   KAITLIN: Are there any flashlights, Ms. Grundy?
4   MS. GRUNDY: I think there's one in the desk over
5   there ...
6   *(KAITLIN pulls a flashlight from the desk drawer.)*
7   MS. PINCHFORK: Well, folks, even in the light there
8   won't be anything to see but a broken down, rusty
9   old building that will cost a fortune to bring up to
10   code!
11   EUNICE: Fortune! Isn't there supposed to be a fortune
12   hidden in here somewhere?
13   MS. PINCHFORK: Mrs. Davenport, do you really
14   believe Cornelius Carter would have hidden
15   anything in a library? He never even learned to
16   read!
17   MS. GRUNDY: But that's why he left the library! He
18   didn't want young people to struggle through life
19   like he had to.
20   ALISTER: *(To MS. GRUNDY)* I suppose you've searched
21   for this fortune?
22   MS. GRUNDY: Me? Heavens, no!
23   EMILY: But the Save the Library Committee has.
24   ALICE: It was one of our first ideas.
25   KAITLIN: Yeah ... find the fortune and save the
26   library.
27   MONICA: I will say, you girls are certainly committed.
28   MS. PINCHFORK: Anybody who doesn't see the
29   potential of demolishing this place ought to be
30   committed!
31   MS. GRUNDY: Ms. Pinchfork!
32   ALISTER: She's got a point! I haven't seen anything
33   that would make me want to invest a dime of the
34   taxpayer's dollars into renovating this dump.
35   KAITLIN: Here! *(She snaps on the flashlight.)* Just have

1 a good look around! Look at the designs in the
2 woodwork!
3 EMILY: And the fireplace! It's real marble!
4 ALICE: And the bookshelf with the mysterious designs
5 on it!
6 MONICA: *(Terrified)* And the body!
7 EUNICE: What body?
8 MONICE: *(Pointing to SAUL's body)* That body!
9 *(ALICE, KAITLIN, and EMILY scream as the lights*
10 *black out and curtain falls.)*
11
12 Scene Four
13
14 *The library, an hour later.*
15 *(AT RISE: SAUL's body is gone. FORTUNE stands at*
16 *Center. MS. GRUNDY, EMILY, ALICE, KAITLIN,*
17 *ALISTER, MONICA, EUNICE, and MS. PINCHFORK*
18 *stand or sit around. CORNELIUS sits in chair at*
19 *Center.)*
20 CORNELIUS: I'm just the caretaker. I don't know who
21 that guy was!
22 FORTUNE: You don't know what he was doing in
23 here?
24 CORNELIUS: No way.
25 FORTUNE: You didn't let him in?
26 CORNELIUS: I was downstairs asleep. I hit the hay
27 early. Big day tomorrow job hunting.
28 EMILY: Maybe not! The planning commission hasn't
29 voted yet.
30 ALISTER: After what's just happened, I don't think we
31 have any choice but to bring this place down.
32 MS. GRUNDY: But that man had nothing to do with
33 the library!
34 MS. PINCHFORK: He was obviously a ... a ... vagrant.
35 And that's what's going to happen with an old,

1   abandoned building like this. It'll become a refuge
2   for ... who knows what kind of people!
3   MS. GRUNDY: It wouldn't be abandoned if the city
4   council hadn't condemned it on Ms. Pinchfork's
5   recommendation.
6   FORTUNE: Ladies! I'm not here to listen to you two
7   squabbling. There's been a murder here!
8   EMILY: Murder!
9   ALISTER: Are you certain that man was murdered,
10   Detective Fortune?
11   FORTUNE: Shot once with a twenty-two caliber
12   handgun.
13   MONICA: *(Frightened)* Oh, dear!
14   FORTUNE: Somethin' wrong, Ms. Harvey?
15   MONICA: Nothing! Nothing at all!
16   *(FORTUNE snaps her purse from her.)*
17   FORTUNE: How about I have a little look?
18   MONICA: Do I have a choice?
19   *(FORTUNE pulls a gun from MONICA's purse.)*
20   ALICE: A twenty-two!
21   FORTUNE: How'd you know it was a twenty-two?
22   ALICE: *(Terrified)* Because ... because ... in any good
23   detective story ... it'd be a twenty-two.
24   MONICA: But it's not what you think! I only carry it
25   for protection. I'm a realtor and have to show
26   houses on my own ... and you never know ...
27   FORTUNE: We'll just put this away for safekeeping. *(He*
28   *pockets the gun.)*
29   MONICA: I didn't hurt anybody! I didn't even know
30   the man.
31   MS. GRUNDY: None of us did!
32   FORTUNE: The victim's name was Slaughter. Saul
33   Slaughter.
34   CORNELIUS: Never heard of him!
35   FORTUNE: You decided that very quickly, Mr. Crump.

1   CORNELIUS: I'd remember somebody with a name
2   like Slaughter, wouldn't you?
3   MS. GRUNDY: I haven't heard of him, either.
4   MONICA: Doesn't ring any bells ...
5   ALISTER: Not with me, either.
6   EMILY: What was he doing in the library?
7   FORTUNE: Probably detecting. He was a private eye.
8   Operated out of Burlington.
9   KAITLIN: That's over fifty miles away.
10   FORTUNE: Probably on a job right here in Carterville.
11   And he must have found something in here.
12   MS. GRUNDY: I hardly think he'd find anything in the
13   library.
14   EMILY: Wait a second ... he had a pencil in his hand,
15   didn't he?
16   ALICE: And a small notepad was lying next to him.
17   MONICE: Had he written anything down, Detective?
18   FORTUNE: You mean like the name of his killer?
19   ALISTER: We wouldn't be having to hang around here
20   if he had, Detective.
21   FORTUNE: Unfortunately he couldn't have written
22   anything. He was dead before he hit the floor.
23   MS. PINCHFORK: Well, then, you'll just have to do
24   your own detecting, Detective Fortune. And
25   perhaps you'll let us all get on our way seeing as
26   how the planning commissioners and I certainly
27   had nothing to do with this horrible crime!
28   EMILY: Well, we didn't, either!
29   CORNELIUS: And I was asleep! Right where I'd like to
30   be now ... *(CORNELIUS yawns and falls asleep.)*
31   FORTUNE: Look, people, calm down or I'll haul you
32   all to headquarters for questioning!
33   ALISTER: Well, question, then!
34   FORTUNE: Any idea what this Saul Slaughter was
35   looking for here?

1 MONICA: Wouldn't it be best if you found out who his
2   client was and then ask him?
3 FORTUNE: You sure it was a *him*, lady?
4 MONICA: Or her.
5 FORTUNE: Detectives don't keep records of things like
6   that ... especially if a client wants to keep it a
7   secret.
8 ALISTER: Well, I didn't hire this Slaughter fellow for
9   anything. Anyone else admit to hiring him?
10   *(ALL look one to another sheepishly.)*
11 EMILY: Maybe ... maybe he was working on his own
12   ... looking for the treasure!
13 FORTUNE: What treasure?
14 MS. GRUNDY: Detective Fortune, you've lived in
15   Carterville all your life. Every year the local paper
16   runs an article and contest on "Where's Carter's
17   Treasure?" You must know about the rumors.
18 FORTUNE: I deal in facts, lady ... not rumors.
19 MS. GRUNDY: If you'd ever come to the library
20   yourself, you'd know that legend has it Mr. Carter
21   hid his fortune somewhere in this building.
22 MS. PINCHFORK: *(To MS. GRUNDY)* One reason you're
23   standing in the way of progress!
24 MS. GRUNDY: Frankly, I don't believe in the treasure,
25   but what else could that man have been looking
26   for?
27 FORTUNE: If there's a fortune here, it's in the walls or
28   under the floor. This place is pretty well emptied
29   out.
30 MS. GRUNDY: Thanks to a certain land-grabbing,
31   money-hungry developer!
32 MS. PINCHFORK: I don't have to take that! Detective,
33   arrest that woman for slander!
34 FORTUNE: Hold on, Ms. Pinchfork! You can't arrest
35   anybody for slander.

1 MS. GRUNDY: Exactly! When the shoe fits —
2 FORTUNE: But you can sue 'em for everything they're
3   worth.
4 MS. GRUNDY: Well, I'm afraid I'm not worth anything
5   at the moment. I don't even have a job, so I
6   couldn't have hired a detective. I could only have
7   paid him in used paperbacks.
8 ALICE: Wait a second ...
9 ALISTER: We've been waiting long enough!
10 KAITLIN: Cornelius is already back asleep.
11 FORTUNE: All right! All right! I'm going to let you all
12   go home for tonight ... but I want you to give the
13   officer by the door your addresses and phone
14   numbers ... and don't any of you plan to leave
15   town.
16 MONICA: I wouldn't think of it! This is my busiest
17   month! *(MONICA pulls out her cellphone, dials, exits*
18   *Right.)*
19 ALISTER: Ms. Pinchfork ... we'll see you at the
20   meeting tomorrow?
21 MS. PINCHFORK: I'll be all set to dot our I's and cross
22   our T's. *(ALISTER and MS. PINCHFORK exit Right.)*
23 EUNICE: Oh, my ... now that I look at this old
24   building ... I see it does have a certain charm. A
25   pity ... such a pity. *(EUNICE exits Right.)*
26 FORTUNE: It's got about as much charm as a
27   mausoleum! *(FORTUNE moves Left, calls out.)* Hey,
28   you guys find anything in that wing? *(He exits Left.)*
29 MS. GRUNDY: Cornelius? Wake up!
30 CORNELIUS: Did they find out who did it?
31 MS. GRUNDY: Not yet, I'm afraid. But you'd better get
32   a good night's sleep so you can find another job
33   tomorrow morning. I'm afraid our plan didn't
34   work out too well. The planning commissioners
35   weren't very impressed.

1 CORNELIUS: Well, I don't think this place was
2   impressed by them, either! 'Night, Ms. Grundy.
3   *(CORNELIUS shuffles Off Left.)*
4 MS. GRUNDY: *(Sighing)* Well, girls ... I guess we should
5   all call it a night. And tomorrow I'll turn over the
6   keys to Ms. Pinchfork.
7 EMILY: You can't do that!
8 ALICE: We haven't begun to fight!
9 MS. GRUNDY: But we're out of ammunition.
10 KAITLIN: There's got to be something we can do!
11 MS. GRUNDY: Have a good cry. 'Night, girls. *(MS.
12   GRUNDY exits Right.)*
13 EMILY: You can't give up, Ms. Grundy! Maybe there is
14   a treasure! *(FORTUNE enters Left.)*
15 FORTUNE: Hey! This is a crime scene! Scram!
16 ALICE: 'Night, Detective! *(EMILY, KAITLIN, and ALICE
17   exit Right. FORTUNE moves to the spot where SAUL
18   fell and examines the bookcase carefully as curtain
19   falls.)*
20
21   **Scene Five**
22
23 *The library, the following dawn.*
24   *(AT RISE: CORNELIUS polishes the librarian's desk
25   and is also examining it very closely, as if looking for
26   something. He hears voices Right, exits Left quickly.
27   EMILY, KAITLIN, and ALICE enter Right, nervously.)*
28 KAITLIN: I've never broken and entered before!
29 ALICE: We also crossed crime scene tape.
30 EMILY: I'm just glad that window was open. Otherwise
31   we'd have had to break it and that would be
32   vandalism.
33 ALICE: This building's condemned, Emily.
34 KAITLIN: Are you sure we're going to get an A for all
35   this effort?

1 EMILY: No, but we might just save the library.
2 KAITLIN: That's stupid! There's no treasure!
3 ALICE: Maybe there is.
4 KAITLIN: Now Emily's got you believing it, too?
5 ALICE: Something's bothered me since we found that
6   poor man last night. He was a detective, right?
7 EMILY: Right.
8 ALICE: And that means he must have been here on a
9   case.
10 KAITLIN: So?
11 ALICE: Then wouldn't it stand to reason he was
12   murdered because he found something?
13 KAITLIN: Oh, Alice, he could have been killed because
14   of another case he was working on ... or maybe it
15   was just a horrible mistake ... or ...
16 EMILY: Or maybe he found something by this
17   bookcase. It's right where he was standing.
18   *(EMILY stares at the bookcase with the numbers, dots,*
19   *and hyphens on it.)*
20 ALICE: And I'll bet he'd written something down on
21   that notepad.
22 KAITLIN: Detective Fortune said he didn't. Emily, why
23   are you staring at the bookcase with the
24   Phoenician symbols on it?
25 ALICE: Phoenician symbols? How'd you know that?
26 KAITLIN: Ms. Steele, my third grade teacher told us
27   about it.
28 ALICE: They just look like random dots and hyphens
29   and numbers to me.
30 KAITLIN: Ms. Steele knew everything.
31 EMILY: Except where the treasure was.
32 KAITLIN: Will you two stop about the treasure? There
33   isn't any treasure! Someone would have found it
34   by now.
35 ALICE: *(Examining the bookcase closely)* **Something's**

1   funny about this design. It looks like it should be
2   so easy ... but I can't get a handle on it. *(Reading)*
3   Five dot hyphen dot hyphen thirteen dot hyphen
4   dot ten. The highest number's thirteen. Make any
5   sense to you?
6 EMILY: Morse code?
7 KAITLIN: How about King Tut's social security
8   number?
9 EMILY: Shhh! Somebody's coming!
10 KAITLIN: The cops! We're in for it now!
11   *(ALICE moves behind librarian's desk.)*
12 ALICE: Get over here and hide!
13   *(EMILY, KAITLIN, and ALICE hide behind the desk.*
14   *MS. GRUNDY enters Right, looks nervously around the*
15   *room. She moves to bookcase. CORNELIUS enters Left.)*
16 CORNELIUS: Mornin', Ms. Grundy!
17 MRS. GRUNDY: Cornelius! You startled me!
18 CORNELIUS: We're not supposed to be here.
19 MS. GRUNDY: I thought you were going job hunting
20   today.
21 CORNELIUS: Looks like you're doing a bit of hunting
22   yourself.
23 MS. GRUNDY: Well, I can't say hope doesn't spring
24   eternal.
25 CORNELIUS: Well, Ma'am, hope you're lucky.
26 MS. GRUNDY: You, too. Finding a job, I mean.
27   *(CORNELIUS exits Right, looking back suspiciously at*
28   *MS. GRUNDY.)* Oh, dear ... *(To portrait)* Mr. Carter,
29   you make me so mad!
30 KAITLIN: *(From behind desk)* Well, you're no peach
31   yourself! *(MS. GRUNDY screams as KAITLIN,*
32   *ALICE, and EMILY rise from behind desk.)* Sorry, Ms.
33   Grundy ... I couldn't resist.
34 MS. GRUNDY: And what are you doing here, girls?
35 EMILY: Probably the same thing you are.

1 MS. GRUNDY: I came ... to ... clean out my desk.
2 ALICE: There's nothing left in the library, Ms. Grundy.
3 MS. GRUNDY: Except the treasure. Are you looking,
4   too?
5 EMILY: Yeah ... it's our last chance before they tear
6   the place down!
7 MS. GRUNDY: You know? I read the last chapter of my
8   biography of Cornelius Carter last night, and the
9   author specifically says that not a penny of
10   Carter's supposed fortune was ever found after his
11   death.
12 KAITLIN: Maybe he spent every cent before he died.
13 ALICE: Yeah ... I'm good at spending every cent I've
14   got.
15 MS. GRUNDY: No ... it's not right. And I just don't
16   think he'd stand by and allow a bulldozer to bring
17   his dream to an end.
18   *(MS. PINCHFORK and FORTUNE enter Right.)*
19 FORTUNE: My apologies, Ms. Pinchfork!
20 MS. PINCHFORK: I told you she sneaked in here! With
21   her accomplices!
22 KAITLIN: *(Pointing to EMILY and ALICE)* They *made* me
23   come! They dragged me!
24 FORTUNE: You crossed a crime scene tape, ladies.
25 MS. GRUNDY: Oh, is *that* what that yellow tape was? I
26   thought it was something the demolition team put
27   up.
28 MS. PINCHFORK: They'll be here tomorrow morning,
29   seven sharp!
30 MS. GRUNDY: Which is why we wanted to take a last
31   look.
32 FORTUNE: Exactly what were you looking for?
33 MS. PINCHFORK: Still hoping you'll find the fortune?
34 ALICE: Well, certain facts point to its existence.
35 FORTUNE: Yeah? Like what?

1 EMILY: *(Covering)* It's all just silly stuff. We didn't really
2   have any business here.
3 FORTUNE: But what'd you find?
4 EMILY: Nothing! And we weren't about to rip the place
5   up board by board.
6 MS. PINCHFORK: Why don't I believe you?
7 FORTUNE: You're always by this bookcase.
8 MS. PINCHFORK: This is right where the body was
9   found.
10 FORTUNE: What is it about this bookcase? Pretty
11   strange design on the edges.
12 KAITLIN: Phoenician designs. That's what my third
13   grade teacher said.
14 MS. PINCHFORK: Well, Detective, I can't keep my eye
15   on this place for the next twenty-four hours, so I
16   hope you'll have a man posted outside. It seems
17   necessary!
18 MS. GRUNDY: The place isn't yours yet, Ms. Pinchfork!
19 MS. PINCHFORK: It's just a matter of three "aye"
20   votes. And I'm off to count the ballots now. *(MS.*
21   *PINCHFORK exits Right.)*
22 EMILY: I guess you're going to arrest us, Detective?
23 FORTUNE: I ought to.
24 EMILY: *(Holding out her hands)* Then go ahead! I can see
25   the *Carterville Chronicle* headline now: "Librarian
26   and Save the Library Committee arrested for
27   taking one last look!"
28 FORTUNE: Get lost! All of you! And I don't want to see
29   you hanging around here again.
30 MS. GRUNDY: Oh, Detective, did you learn anything
31   more about Mr. Slaughter?
32 ALICE: Like the name of his client?
33 FORTUNE: His secretary said she only knew it was
34   somebody in Carterville ... but he wouldn't even
35   tell her who it was.

1   EMILY: Man or woman?

2   FORTUNE: She couldn't tell over the phone. The voice

3   was disguised.

4   EMILY: Spooky!

5   FORTUNE: Yeah? Well, bein' a private eye's a

6   dangerous business.

7   MS. GRUNDY: Good luck, Detective.

8   ALICE: Hope you get your man.

9   KAITLIN: Or woman. *(MS. GRUNDY, EMILY, and*

10   *KAITLIN exit Right. ALICE keeps staring at the*

11   *bookcase.)*

12   FORTUNE: What do you see that I can't see?

13   ALICE: Hmmm? Oh, nothing. Nothing at all. *(ALICE*

14   *runs Off Right. FORTUNE pulls notepad SAUL had*

15   *been writing on in Scene One from his pocket and looks*

16   *from it to the bookcase as the curtain falls.)*

17

18   Scene Six

19

20   *The street across from the library that night.*

21   *Played in front of the curtain.*

22   *(AT RISE: ALICE, EMILY, and KAITLIN enter Left.*

23   *They carry flashlights.)*

24   ALICE: Hurry up before it rains!

25   *(Sound of thunder)*

26   KAITLIN: If we're caught in the library again, we'll be

27   arrested for sure!

28   EMILY: Oh, Kaitlin, who'll catch us? Do you see a

29   patrol car guarding the building?

30   KAITLIN: Well, somebody's supposed to be guarding

31   it! Ms. Pinchfork demanded it.

32   EMILY: It doesn't matter now. The planning commission

33   voted to demolish the building.

34   ALICE: And I'm sure Detective Fortune's done inside.

35   I've just got to get one last look.

1   KAITLIN: Why?
2   ALICE: I figured something out! The highest number
3   on the bookcase was thirteen, right? Doesn't that
4   mean anything to you?
5   KAITLIN: Yeah! It's unlucky, and we're going to be
6   unlucky if we go in there again!
7   ALICE: Do I have to spell it out in black and white?
8   EMILY: How about just letters. Plain old letters.
9   ALICE: That's exactly the point! Come on! *(ALICE and*
10   *EMILY exit Right.)*
11 KAITLIN: *(Thinking)* Wait a second! *What* exactly is the
12   point? *(KAITLIN exits Right. MS. PINCHFORK*
13   *enters, pulls out a cellphone, and dials.)*
14 PINCHFORK: *(Into phone)* I think we've got a problem!
15   *(Lights out.)*
16
17   Scene Seven
18
19 *The library, immediately after.*
20   *(AT RISE: The stage is dimly lit. ALICE, EMILY, and*
21   *KAITLIN enter nervously Right holding flashlights*
22   *which are turned on.)*
23 ALICE: Ms. Grundy's supposed to meet us here.
24 EMILY: It's ten on the dot.
25   *(MS. GRUNDY enters Left.)*
26 MS. GRUNDY: And I'm here, girls. What have you
27   figured out?
28 KAITLIN: That we're all going to do ten to twenty for
29   breaking and entering.
30 EMILY: They couldn't give us a sentence like that.
31 KAITLIN: It's our second offense!
32 ALICE: Ms. Grundy ... this writing on the bookcase is
33   a code.
34 MS. GRUNDY: I never thought it really meant
35   anything.

40

1 EMILY: Math genius here figured it out.
2 ALICE: It's so simple!
3 KAITLIN: To a genius!
4 ALICE: How many letters are there in the alphabet?
5 KAITLIN: Twenty-six.
6 ALICE: So whoever designed the code gave the first
7   thirteen letters a value of positive one to thirteen
8   and the second thirteen letters a value of negative
9   one to thirteen.
10 KAITLIN: *(Confused)* Oh, *that* makes sense!
11 ALICE: Or vice versa.
12 MS. GRUNDY: I think I see what you mean.
13 EMILY: Let's try it.
14 ALICE: I've written the alphabet out two different
15   ways. Let's see which one fits.
16 EMILY: *(Reading from the bookcase edge)* **Five dot**
17   **hyphen nine.**
18 ALICE: Five dot negative nine. No, that won't work.
19   The negatives must be the first thirteen letters not
20   the second. If we do it that way, five dot negative
21   nine spells R-E.
22 EMILY: *(Reading)* Negative thirteen dot negative ten
23   dot negative five dot one dot negative seven.
24 KAITLIN: What's that spell?
25 ALICE: Reading!
26 MS. GRUNDY: Oh, my goodness! All this time ... and
27   no one ever took the trouble to notice!
28 EMILY: Sometimes it just takes a crisis.
29 KAITLIN: What else does it say?
30 ALICE: *(Scribbling and working)* "Reading ... will ... lift
31   ... the ..."
32 KAITLIN: The what? The what?
33 ALICE: Just a second! *(Scribbles more.)*
34 MS. GRUNDY: There must be a treasure, then!
35 KAITLIN: But all it talks about is reading.

1 ALICE: *(Triumphantly)* "Reading will lift the mantel of
2   ignorance."
3 MS. GRUNDY: *(Sighing)* What a wonderful thought!
4 KAITLIN: It doesn't tell where the treasure is.
5 EMILY: *(Thinking)* Well, we just *read* something.
6 KAITLIN: And there's a *mantel*. So what?
7 ALICE: *Lift* the mantel!
8 MS. GRUNDY: Do you suppose — *(MS. GRUNDY tries to*
9   *lift the mantel. When she fails, the girls help. Finally it*
10   *flips up.)*
11 ALICE: It worked!
12 KAITLIN: What's in here? What is it?
13 MS. GRUNDY: Something in an envelope. *(She pulls an*
14   *envelope from under the mantel top.)* It's just an
15   envelope ...
16 KAITLIN: And with our luck it's empty!
17   *(FORTUNE and MS. PINCHFORK enter Right.)*
18 FORTUNE: And your luck's run out!
19 MS. PINCHFORK: Snooping again, ladies? I just can't
20   let you out of my sight, can I?
21 FORTUNE: I'll take the envelope.
22 MS. GRUNDY: It belongs to the library, Detective.
23 FORTUNE: It's evidence.
24 ALICE: It doesn't have anything to do with the crime.
25 FORTUNE: Oh, no? Saul Slaughter was killed for it.
26 EMILY: Nobody knows that for certain.
27 ALICE: *(Suspiciously)* Except the killer.
28 FORTUNE: Hand it over!
29 MS. GRUNDY: Actually, I don't think there's anything
30   in there.
31 MS. PINCHFORK: I kept telling you, there never was
32   a treasure!
33 EMILY: But there must be something important for Old
34   Man Carter to have hidden it so carefully.
35 FORTUNE: Hand it over!

1 MS. PINCHFORK: Oh, Detective, just arrest them and
2   get them out of here!
3 FORTUNE: *(Pulling rope from his pocket)* **Here, Ms.**
4   **Pinchfork, tie them up.**
5 MS. PINCHFORK: Why?
6 FORTUNE: What time's the wrecking crew coming?
7 MS. PINCHFORK: Seven.
8 FORTUNE: It's a wait, but I'll just give them the all-
9   clear.
10 EMILY: I don't like the sound of this.
11 FORTUNE: Tie them up, Ms. Pinchfork! *(FORTUNE*
12   *draws a gun from his pocket.)*
13 MS. PINCHFORK: Detective, how *dare* you pull a gun
14   on me!
15 ALICE: That's Ms. Harvey's gun!
16 EMILY: I think we've all made a big mistake. You
17   killed Saul Slaughter, didn't you, Detective
18   Fortune? You're the client from Carterville!
19 FORTUNE: I've wanted that treasure for years! Ever
20   since I came across a letter from Carter to his
21   lawyer ... it was in another case I was working on
22   ... and he mentions no one would find anything of
23   his fortune because he sunk it all into one last
24   investment he hid in the library for safekeeping.
25   He figured the library would be here forever, the
26   old fool!
27 MS. PINCHFORK: So once I decided to put a mall up
28   here ... and the library was coming down ...
29 FORTUNE: I had to move fast, right? I hired
30   Slaughter, and we were supposed to meet here
31   and figure the thing out. But I got here a little
32   early and found out he was going to double-cross
33   me!
34 MS. GRUNDY: But you hadn't found the treasure.
35 FORTUNE: But I could tell if anybody could find it ...

1 these three could! *(To MS. PINCHFORK)* Now tie
2 'em up! It's gonna be such a shame when they tear
3 this place down and nobody knew you were in it.
4 MS. PINCHFORK: I won't help you do anything!
5 FORTUNE: Then you gotta suffer the consequences,
6 lady!
7 *(CORNELIUS pops up from behind the librarian's desk*
8 *and hits FORTUNE over the head with a mop. MS.*
9 *PINCHFORK grabs the gun as FORTUNE falls.)*
10 MS. GRUNDY: Cornelius! I'd forgotten you!
11 CORNELIUS: Just doin' my job. Takin' care of things!
12 MS. PINCHFORK: I'll call the police. *(Pulls out*
13 *cellphone.)*
14 EMILY: Yeah ... tell them we've got the killer.
15 ALICE: Maybe we ought to tie him up 'til backup
16 arrives.
17 KAITLIN: I'll help! *(Using FORTUNE's rope, ALICE and*
18 *KAITLIN tie FORTUNE's hands behind his back.)*
19 MS. PINCHFORK: *(Into phone)* Nine one one? We need
20 the police at the Carterville Library immediately!
21 We've caught the killer. No, I won't tell you ...
22 you'll have to be surprised.
23 CORNELIUS: Now, Ms. Grundy ... I think we ought to
24 take a look in the envelope.
25 EMILY: That's right! The treasure!
26 ALICE: What could be so light, yet worth everything
27 Mr. Carter had?
28 KAITLIN: Maybe it's a check for millions and millions!
29 CORNELIUS: Nobody would cash a check that's a
30 hundred years old.
31 *(MS. GRUNDY pulls a small piece of parchment from*
32 *the envelope.)*
33 MS. GRUNDY: Oh! Oh, my goodness! *(Shaken, MS.*
34 *GRUNDY sits on chair.)*
35 MS. PINCHFORK: Whatever it is, it's not enough to

1   save this library.
2 MS. GRUNDY: No? It's a small legal notice ...
3 MS. PINCHFORK: We've done everything as legally as
4   possible.
5 MS. GRUNDY: ... signed by William Shakespeare.
6 ALICE: Shakespeare's signature?
7 MS. GRUNDY: There are only five known pieces of
8   Shakespeare's handwriting in existence. This
9   makes six.
10 KAITLIN: Not nearly as exciting as diamonds.
11 MS. GRUNDY: But it's priceless!
12 MS. PINCHFORK: You mean I've been bought out by
13   Shakespeare?
14 EMILY: I don't think you can afford this piece of
15   property now, Ms. Pinchfork.
16 *(MS. PINCHFORK dials her cellphone.)*
17 MS. PINCHFORK: *(Into phone)* Al? Listen, about that
18   wrecking contract for today. Cancel it. We're going
19   back to the drawing board!
20 *(GIRLS cheer as the curtain falls.)*

The Mermaid

Synopsis:
Two sisters become greedy when their fisherman brother
catches a mermaid. Can they carry out their crafty plan before
the mystery of the mermaid is solved?

Characters (3 male, 4 female):
ABEL BUNDAGE, late teens, a fisherman
CORA BUNDAGE, early twenties, his sister
BITTY BUNDAGE, mid twenties, another sister
THE MERMAID, about twenty
JEAN LATOUR, a pirate
HACKSAW, another pirate
OLD WOMAN

Setting:
The Bundage cottage located in another country, in an earlier
time. We see a cabin-like room with wing entrances Down Left
and Right. Window Up Center. Table and chairs Right Center;
fireplace with pot hanging over fire Left Center. Scattered
fishing equipment here and there about the simple, almost
austere room.

Props:
Coins; jar; pot hanging above fireplace; ladle in pot; mug;
blanket; elaborate ring; two fancy hats; broom; bucket and rag;
piece of bread; key; rope.

Costumes:
Long dresses for female characters. Mermaid's dress is torn and
dirty. Old woman wears shawl. Long-sleeve, plain shirts for all
male characters along with long, dark pants and boots. Vests are
fine as are sailing caps or hats.

1	**Scene One**
2	*The cottage, evening.*
3	*(AT RISE: BITTY stands at window looking out.*
4	*CORA sits at table emptying a few coins from a jar.)*
5	**CORA:** What's our baby brother doing now?
6	**BITTY:** Talking to the few fish he caught. Probably
7	apologizing to 'em!
8	**CORA:** He's crazy. You know that.
9	**BITTY:** I know it. Mama always said it came from his
10	rolling out of his crib one night and having the
11	dog sit on his head 'til dawn.
12	**CORA:** At least Mama had the good sense to die before
13	she had to rely on him to make a decent day's
14	catch.
15	**BITTY:** What have we got there?
16	**CORA:** Five shillings, six pence.
17	**BITTY:** *(Disappointed)* That's not enough!
18	**CORA:** *(Dropping money back into jar, rising)* You'd think
19	he'd have the decency to want his sisters decked
20	out in new hats once in a while.
21	**BITTY:** We need eight shillings for just one hat.
22	**CORA:** What good is one hat for the two of us?
23	**BITTY:** I could wear it one day to the village, and you
24	could wear it the next.
25	**CORA:** *(Pouting)* But everyone would have seen it! I
26	want my own new hat!
27	**BITTY:** Oh, it's just not fair being condemned to live
28	like this!
29	**CORA:** We work and slave just to make a pleasant
30	home, and all he does is spit in the sea!
31	*(ABEL enters Right.)*
32	**ABEL:** Evenin' sisters. *(He sniffs around.)*
33	**BITTY:** What are you doin'?
34	**ABEL:** Thought I might catch a whiff of supper
35	cookin'.

1   BITTY: Supper? We ate ours. It got late, and we got
2   hungry.
3   CORA: You can't expect us to wait 'til dark falls!
4   ABEL: Then would it be too much trouble to heat up
5   what's left?
6   BITTY: There ain't much. *(Moves to fireplace to begin*
7   *stirring pot.)* Just scrapings from the bottom.
8   CORA: On account of your not catchin' many fish,
9   Abel.
10   ABEL: But today, dear sisters, my luck changed.
11   CORA: *(Sarcastically)* Must have been all that spittin'
12   into the sea you did this morning.
13   ABEL: Must have been. Mortimer Crutch told me that
14   if you spit into the sea the morning after a storm,
15   you'll have a lucky catch.
16   BITTY: What would that old fool know?
17   CORA: *(To ABEL)* Are you sayin' you caught more than
18   a couple of mackerel?
19   ABEL: I caught the most wonderful thing a sailor can
20   catch — a mermaid!
21   BITTY: I do believe he's lost his mind, sister Cora.
22   CORA: We'd better call the doctor.
23   ABEL: I know it's hard to believe, but she's right
24   outside the door.
25   BITTY: There's a mermaid on the porch?
26   ABEL: Uh-huh!
27   CORA: *(Sarcastically)* Oh, your mermaid can live out of
28   water, Abel?
29   ABEL: Seems to do just fine.
30   BITTY: So will we be able to sell this mermaid at the
31   market to make some money?
32   ABEL : No! *(ABEL exits Right.)*
33   CORA: *(Calling after him)* Well, if we can't sell her at the
34   market maybe we could send her off to a circus so
35   they can exhibit her. A shilling a peek! *(CORA and*

1   *BITTY laugh.)*
2   BITTY: Sister, we're going to have to do something
3   about our baby brother!
4   *(ABEL enters Right with MERMAID, dressed in torn*
5   *clothing, her hair bedraggled. She is wrapped in a*
6   *blanket. She cannot talk. On her right hand she wears*
7   *a beautiful ring. CORA and BITTY watch with*
8   *growing amusement as ABEL gently helps MERMAID*
9   *to chair where she can sit. They suddenly burst out*
10   *laughing again.)*
11   CORA: This is your mermaid?
12   BITTY: Where are her flippers?
13   CORA: And she ain't exactly a beauty!
14   BITTY: She's more like a beast!
15   CORA: Abel, where did you find this ... this ...
16   creature?
17   ABEL: She was clinging to a piece of wood, struggling
18   for life.
19   BITTY: Pretty used to strugglin', I'd say. Where are
20   you from, girl?
21   *(No response)*
22   CORA: Oh, she's the coy type. Answer us, girl! What
23   were you doing in the sea?
24   ABEL: It's no use, sisters. The mermaid doesn't talk.
25   She's not said a single word since I pulled her
26   from the water. *(ABEL gives MERMAID a mug of*
27   *soup, which she eats hungrily.)*
28   BITTY: Ain't that convenient!
29   CORA: But she sure comes with an appetite!
30   ABEL: You watch her while I go get the fish unloaded.
31   BITTY: Oh, so you did bring home something we can
32   sell!
33   ABEL: Aye. She was my last catch of the day. *(ABEL*
34   *exits Right.)*
35   CORA: And what are we supposed to do with a

1   mermaid, Bitty?

2   BITTY: There's barely enough food for the three of us.

3   And now he brings in a flea-bag with the appetite

4   of a horse!

5   CORA: *(Grabbing MERMAID's hand)* But look at this

6   ring! Maybe it'll fetch a few shillings. *(She pulls ring*

7   *off MERMAID's hand as the curtain falls.)*

8

9   **Scene Two**

10

11   *Midday, the following day.*

12   *(AT RISE: MERMAID sits at table, seemingly unaware*

13   *of where she is. ABEL brings her a mug of tea from*

14   *fireplace.)*

15   ABEL: Here's some tea. Drink it. It'll make you feel

16   better. *(No response)* I'm going to find your family

17   as soon as my sisters return. I'm going to every

18   village along the coast to find out who you belong

19   to. I'll find out what happened. I'll get you home.

20   Except there are a lot of villages. It may take 'til

21   tonight or even tomorrow.

22   *(CORA and BITTY enter Right each wearing a new*

23   *hat.)*

24   CORA: I really like mine the best!

25   BITTY: But mine has more ribbons!

26   CORA: Abel! What are you doing home at this hour?

27   BITTY: You've missed the best fishing of the day!

28   ABEL: Where did you get those new hats?

29   CORA: The millinery shop, where else?

30   BITTY: We were tired of looking so lackluster.

31   ABEL: So now we owe the millinery shop money.

32   CORA: Oh, no! We —

33   BITTY: *(Covering)* We set a bit aside.

34   CORA: But you haven't told us what you're doing

35   home, Abel.

1 ABEL: I didn't want to leave the Mermaid alone. But
2   now that you're back from the village, I'll be on
3   my way.
4 BITTY: What good is it at this hour? There's nothing
5   left to catch.
6 ABEL: I'm not going fishing. Not until I find the
7   Mermaid's family.
8 CORA: You're not going fishing?
9 BITTY: Do you realize how hard it will be to find her
10   family?
11 ABEL: Someone must be missing her. She's too kind
12   and beautiful to be alone in the world.
13 CORA: So she's told you that?
14 ABEL: Not in words.
15 BITTY: Abel, you're crazy! You're not going to waste
16   your day going from door to door asking people if
17   they lost a mermaid!
18 ABEL: I'll lose a day, a week, a month. Whatever it
19   takes!
20 CORA: And what are we supposed to do in the
21   meantime?
22 ABEL: Care for her. *(Exits Right.)*
23 BITTY: Care for her?
24 CORA: *(Nastily)* But we don't care for her!
25 BITTY: We don't have any room for an intruder!
26 CORA: Unless they earn their keep.
27 BITTY: That's right! *(BITTY grabs a broom and thrusts it*
28   *at MERMAID.)* Here! You can sweep up the floor!
29 CORA: Sweep! Or we'll take a switch to you! *(CORA*
30   *slams her fist on table. MERMAID jumps.)*
31 BITTY: Take the broom and sweep! *(MERMAID takes*
32   *the broom.)* Now, sweep!
33   *(CORA again slams her fist on table. MERMAID*
34   *begins to sweep.)*
35 CORA: That's right!

1 BITTY: It appears, sister, maybe we've got ourselves a
2   servant!
3   *(The curtain falls.)*
4
5   **Scene Three**
6
7 *The same, a week later.*
8   *(AT RISE: MERMAID scrubs floor Down Center.*
9   *BITTY hands CORA, who sits at table, a scrap of*
10   *bread.)*
11 BITTY: That's the last of it.
12 CORA: And he's still out there knocking on doors!
13 BITTY: You'd think after a week he'd have given up!
14 CORA: Especially with no food left in the house.
15 BITTY: Maybe we should —
16 CORA: Maybe we should what?
17 BITTY: Return the hats.
18 CORA: How dare you think such a thing! We deserve
19   those hats! And we deserve a lot more! *(CORA rises*
20   *and stands above MERMAID.)* And, sister dear, we're
21   going to get it.
22 BITTY: What are you up to?
23 CORA: There's an old saying, "When life gives you
24   lemons, make lemonade."
25 BITTY: Mr. Granger used to say that all the time at
26   school. I got so sick of it 'cause I hate lemonade.
27 CORA: But lemons are worse. *(Pointing to MERMAID)*
28   And this is the worst lemon we've come across,
29   wouldn't you agree?
30 BITTY: She's made a mess of everything.
31 CORA: I spoke to Damian Drudge yesterday.
32 BITTY: *(Interested)* The thief?
33 CORA: *(Slyly)* Bitty! He merely deals in cast-off goods
34   and unwanted items.
35 BITTY: Why'd you speak to him?

1   CORA: I thought he might be able to help us.
2   BITTY: How?
3   CORA: You see what a fine servant this girl is.
4   BITTY: Very thorough.
5   CORA: And how obedient she is! *(CORA knocks on the*
6   *table. MERMAID looks at her, terrified.)* **That's**
7   **enough scrubbing, girl! Clean out the fireplace.**
8   *(CORA again knocks on the table. MERMAID moves to*
9   *the fireplace to begin her work.)*
10   BITTY: So easy to train.
11   CORA: People would pay a big price for such a
12   servant. People very far off, of course.
13   BITTY: Mr. Drudge can arrange it?
14   CORA: No, but he gave our name to someone who can.
15   BITTY: Who?
16   CORA: A Captain Jean LaTour.
17   BITTY: He sounds like a pirate!
18   *(A knock is heard Off Right.)*
19   CORA: Shhh! Perhaps it's him! *(CORA knocks on table.)*
20   **Go to the other room! Go!** *(MERMAID exits Left.*
21   *CORA follows her.)*
22   BITTY: Shall I open the door?
23   *(CORA enters Left putting a key in her pocket.)*
24   CORA: She'll not get out. Yes, let Captain LaTour in.
25   *(BITTY exits Right, returns a moment later with OLD*
26   *WOMAN.)*
27   BITTY: Cora, it's not —
28   CORA: Who are you?
29   OLD WOMAN: Oh, please ... may I sit down?
30   BITTY: You're not staying long.
31   OLD WOMAN: *(Sitting)* No ... I can't stay long anywhere.
32   My journey's far from done.
33   CORA: What are you talking about?
34   OLD WOMAN: I am looking for my daughter.
35   BITTY: Your daughter?

1   OLD WOMAN: She was lost at sea a week ago.
2   CORA: Why do you come here?
3   OLD WOMAN: I have gone everywhere along the
4   coast. I've been to every village ... every house. All
5   to no avail.
6   BITTY: Then perhaps your daughter is ... dead.
7   OLD WOMAN: I don't believe that! I can't believe that!
8   CORA: Why not?
9   OLD WOMAN: Something in my heart tells me she's
10   alive. She was returning from the islands where
11   she had gone to visit her aunt for several months.
12   She was on a schooner ... a strong ship ... but it
13   must have been caught in that storm. Miriam's a
14   strong swimmer ... a sensible girl. The only thing
15   is ...
16 BITTY: Yes?
17 OLD WOMAN: She couldn't cry out for help!
18 CORA: Why not?
19 OLD WOMAN: Miriam has never been able to speak.
20   *(BITTY looks nervously at CORA.)*
21 BITTY: But, Cora ...
22 CORA: A heartbreaking tale, Madam ... but you can
23   see we sisters are alone. Our brother is a
24   fisherman, and he is out today, as always.
25 OLD WOMAN: *(Rising, moving to window)* Oh, is that his
26   boat sitting in the sand, drifted in as if it hasn't
27   been used in a week?
28 CORA: *(Covering)* That's ... that's our old boat. He has
29   a new one.
30 OLD WOMAN: *(Looking around the room)* He must do
31   very well indeed.
32 BITTY: Oh, yes. We want for nothing!
33 OLD WOMAN: I am happy for you, then. And I, too,
34   would want for nothing if only I had Miriam!
35   *(Calling)* Miriam! *(A knock is heard Off Left.)* What

1   was that?
2 CORA: Our cat. Your crying out has woken him up.
3 OLD WOMAN: I'm sorry I disturbed him.
4 BITTY: I'm afraid we've been no help to you.
5 OLD WOMAN: But you have!
6 BITTY: *(Terrified)* What do you mean?
7 OLD WOMAN: *(Sweetly)* This is one less cottage I must
8   visit. I thank you for your time.
9 CORA: We wish you luck in finding your daughter. But
10   I'm afraid after a week ...
11 OLD WOMAN: As long as I have breath, I have hope.
12   *(Exits Right.)*
13 BITTY: Oh, Cora! We can't just keep that girl here.
14 CORA: Why not? If we play our cards right, she'll pay
15   for a life of comfort for us.
16 BITTY: But what will we tell Abel if he comes home
17   and his mermaid's gone?
18 CORA: We'll just say her mother came to get her.
19 BITTY: Oh, yes ... I see.
20 CORA: It couldn't have worked out better for us, Bitty!
21   It's almost as if it was preordained that that old
22   hag came by.
23 BITTY: And the girl will be sold to a good home?
24 CORA: Of course! She'll probably be treated as a
25   member of the family. And the best part is ... she'll
26   never be able to tell what happened to her!
27 BITTY: That is a stroke of luck!
28   *(A knock is heard Off Right.)*
29 CORA: *(Moving Right, angrily)* We told you we don't
30   know anything — *(CORA exits Right, returns a*
31   *moment later with JEAN and HACKSAW.)* You'll have
32   to excuse me. We've been in a dispute with our
33   neighbors over some chickens.
34 JEAN: Of course, Madam! We understand, don't we,
35   Hacksaw?

1   HACKSAW: Right!
2   JEAN: I, of course, am Captain Jean LaTour, and this
3   is Hacksaw.
4   CORA: I'm Cora Bundage. *(JEAN kisses CORA's hand,*
5   *much to her embarrassment.)* And this is my sister,
6   Bitty. *(JEAN kisses BITTY's hand.)*
7   JEAN: You have a very lovely place here.
8   BITTY: Oh, it's nothing.
9   HACKSAW: You can say that again! *(JEAN kicks*
10   *HACKSAW.)* Ouch!
11 JEAN: Hacksaw is still learning his manners.
12 CORA: Well, lately things haven't been very prosperous
13   around our village.
14 JEAN: Alas, these terrible pirates are taking a toll on
15   commerce.
16 BITTY: I shiver at the sound of the word.
17 CORA: And this is why I spoke to Mr. Drudge.
18 JEAN: He mentioned something about a servant?
19 CORA: Yes ... a servant who's bound out to us. But we
20   can no longer keep up our side of her ... contract.
21   Our food is so low that we can't afford the extra
22   mouth.
23 JEAN: A pity, eh, Hacksaw?
24 HACKSAW: A real pity!
25 CORA: Mr. Drudge mentioned that perhaps you could
26   find a new place for our poor servant girl?
27 JEAN: It's been done.
28 CORA: Of course the contract would have to be bought
29   out. I mean, having trained her and taken care of
30   her all these years.
31 JEAN: And how many years have you had her?
32 CORA: Five!
33 BITTY: *(Simultaneously with CORA)* Three!
34 CORA: *(Angrily)* It's been five. My poor sister here has
35   what we call failing memory.

1   BITTY: Is that what I have?
2   CORA: It's been five years since Miriam first came to
3   us.
4   BITTY: Time flies!
5   HACKSAW: Maybe we ought to have a look at her.
6   CORA: Bitty, why don't you get Miriam? *(CORA hands*
7   *BITTY the key.)*
8   BITTY: Right away. *(BITTY exits Left.)*
9   CORA: So, Captain LaTour, how much is our ...
10   commission?
11   JEAN: Depending on the girl, twenty pounds.
12   CORA: I won't take a pence less than twenty five!
13   HACKSAW: Twenty-five?! The Captain never —
14   JEAN: Never say never, Hacksaw. I have a family
15   currently looking for someone to help out with the
16   children —
17   *(BITTY enters Left with MERMAID.)*
18   CORA: Here's Miriam now.
19   *(MERMAID reacts to name with fear.)*
20   JEAN: Let's have a look at you!
21   HACKSAW: It's a dirty one, all right.
22   JEAN: Looks a bit waterlogged.
23   CORA: We don't have the money to keep our servants
24   well-groomed!
25   BITTY: Maybe her next family will be able to take
26   better care of her.
27   JEAN: Maybe they will.
28   CORA: One excellent feature is that the girl says
29   nothing.
30   BITTY: She'll never sass or get uppity.
31   CORA: Quiet as a mouse.
32   JEAN: Admirable!
33   CORA: You'll take her, then?
34   JEAN: For twenty-three pounds.
35   CORA: Cash.

1   JEAN: *(Handing over coins)* **Cash!**
2   HACKSAW: **Come along, girly!** *(HACKSAW moves to*
3   *MERMAID, but she backs away.)* **Come along, I say!**
4   *(ABEL enters Right.)*
5   ABEL: **What's going on here?**
6   CORA: **Abel!**
7   BITTY: **You're not due back 'til tonight!**
8   ABEL: *(To JEAN and HACKSAW)* **Who are you?**
9   JEAN: *(Bowing)* **Captain Jean LaTour.**
10 HACKSAW: **And Hacksaw.**
11 CORA: **They're your little mermaid's ... brothers.**
12 BITTY: **Come to fetch her home.**
13 ABEL: **No! No! She doesn't know either of you! I see it**
14   **in her face.**
15 CORA: **Don't be ridiculous, Abel! Of course these men**
16   **are her family. Why, they got wind of your**
17   **traveling about trying to find her people and came**
18   **right over when they heard, didn't you?**
19 JEAN: **Exactly as the lady says. So come along, girly!**
20 HACKSAW: **We ain't gonna hurt you!** *(He grabs*
21   *MERMAID, who struggles.)*
22 ABEL: **You're not taking her anywhere!** *(He dives for*
23   *HACKSAW. They struggle. JEAN strikes ABEL on the*
24   *back of his head. ABEL falls.)*
25 BITTY: **Abel!** *(To JEAN)* **You didn't have to hit him so**
26   **hard.**
27 JEAN: **I don't like people standing in my way, lady.**
28 HACKSAW: **We gets what we want! Now, come on,**
29   **girly! It's time to go!** *(HACKSAW grabs MERMAID as*
30   *JEAN moves to CORA.)*
31 JEAN: **So nice doing business with you!**
32 CORA: **Likewise, I'm sure!**
33   *(JEAN kisses CORA's hand again, then exits Right.*
34   *HACKSAW follows with MERMAID in tow.)*
35 BITTY: **Abel! Wake up, Abel!**

1   CORA: Stop trying to wake him up. Help me tie his
2   hands!
3   BITTY: Cora! We can't tie our brother's hands!
4   CORA: We've got to! He'll race out after them if we
5   don't. It's only 'til Captain LaTour is well out of
6   sight. *(CORA grabs rope and she and BITTY tie*
7   *ABEL's hands.)*
8   BITTY: You got twenty-three pounds?
9   CORA: Isn't it wonderful? It would take a year of
10   fishing to get that much!
11   BITTY: And at the rate Abel's luck has been going, it
12   would take ten years!
13   *(CORA and BITTY laugh. ABEL awakens.)*
14   ABEL: Where is she? What have you done?
15   CORA: Now, Abel, we've done what's best for us all.
16   BITTY: We've got twenty-three pounds.
17   CORA: And your little mermaid is going to a nice
18   home where she'll be a fine servant.
19   ABEL: A servant?! She's no servant! How could you
20   have done this?
21   BITTY: *(Angrily)* Maybe you should have made a better
22   living!
23   CORA: Really! All these years expecting us to live on
24   a few shillings a week.
25   BITTY: You were just too lazy, Abel!
26   CORA: And now it's come back to haunt you.
27   BITTY: But we'll share everything with you.
28   CORA: And you know something? Finding that
29   mermaid did work out to be the luckiest thing
30   you've ever done! *(CORA jingles the coins as OLD*
31   *WOMAN enters Right.)*
32   OLD WOMAN: Excuse me ... I notice your brother has
33   returned.
34   CORA: Go away!
35   BITTY: We're done with you!

1   OLD WOMAN: I don't think so.

2   ABEL: Who are you?

3   OLD WOMAN: I was here a while ago looking for my

4   daughter Miriam who was lost at sea a week ago.

5   Your sisters said she was not here, but ...

6   CORA: Get out of our house!

7   BITTY: You've got no right coming in here like this!

8   ABEL: Your daughter was lost during a storm?

9   OLD WOMAN: That's right. And I've been looking for

10   her ever since. Her name's Miriam.

11   ABEL: Miriam! That's a beautiful name.

12   OLD WOMAN: And she's a beautiful girl, but sadly

13   unable to speak or call for help.

14   ABEL: They've taken her! That captain that was here

15   and his henchman took her off and they're selling

16   her to a family as a servant! Untie me so I can stop

17   them!

18   OLD WOMAN: *(Untying ABEL)* Who would have done

19   such a thing?

20   CORA: *(Grabbing the OLD WOMAN)* Don't you touch

21   him!

22   BITTY: Get out of here! Get out!

23   ABEL: Hurry, or they'll be gone! *(MIRIAM enters Right.)*

24   Miriam! *(ABEL runs to her.)*

25   CORA: You naughty child!

26   BITTY: Go back to Captain LaTour at once!

27   OLD WOMAN: I'm afraid Captain LaTour has no need

28   of my daughter.

29   CORA: Your daughter? Ha! You probably don't have

30   any daughter, you old hag! And if you did, you

31   probably sold her as a servant long ago!

32   OLD WOMAN: *(To her daughter)* My child, how sorry I

33   am you had to suffer so.

34   CORA: *(Grabbing OLD WOMAN)* Get out of our house!

35   BITTY: *(Crying)* You've ruined everything!

1 OLD WOMAN: Remove your hands at once, or I'll have
2   your heads!
3 CORA: Who are you to talk to ladies like that?
4 OLD WOMAN: *(Imperiously)* Lady Ashcroft! My late
5   husband was advisor to his majesty, the king!
6 BITTY: Oh, we've got another crazy one here! *(OLD*
7   *WOMAN breaks away from CORA, then shows her*
8   *ring.)*
9 OLD WOMAN: The royal ring!
10   *(ABEL bows when he sees it.)*
11 ABEL: Lady Ashcroft!
12 BITTY: That ... that ring, Cora ...
13 CORA: Shut up!
14 OLD WOMAN: You sold Miriam's ring, didn't you?
15   That's how I came to know she was here. The ring
16   came into my possession by way of a merchant
17   who recognized it as the royal ring. I came to see
18   what kind of people would treat my daughter so!
19 BITTY: *(Indicating CORA)* It was all *her* idea!
20 CORA: Shut up, Bitty!
21 OLD WOMAN: As if Miriam hasn't had enough sorrow
22   in her life ... you cast her in the role of servant
23   and sold her to Captain LaTour.
24 CORA: We couldn't afford to keep her here.
25 OLD WOMAN: For this you should lose your heads!
26 BITTY: *(Grabbing her neck)* No! Oh, no!
27 ABEL: Please, Lady Ashcroft ... it's all my fault.
28 OLD WOMAN: In what way?
29 ABEL: I found your daughter in the sea.
30 OLD WOMAN: For which I am deeply grateful.
31 ABEL: But I left her every day to search for her
32   family.
33 OLD WOMAN: For which I am also thankful.
34 ABEL: My poor sisters, though, didn't realize who your
35   daughter was.

1 OLD WOMAN: But you didn't, either. Yet you treated
2   her with kindness and respect, and they treated
3   her with scorn and hate.
4 ABEL: Please spare their lives.
5 OLD WOMAN: Only if they leave at once and never
6   return to this land.
7 ABEL: Never return?
8 OLD WOMAN: Never!
9 CORA: Where will we go?
10 BITTY: What will we do?
11 OLD WOMAN: You have money. More money than you
12   ever dreamed from Captain LaTour. Go at once!
13 CORA: This is all your fault, Abel!
14 BITTY: Your lucky day! Ha!
15 CORA: We'll never forgive you for this!
16 BITTY: Mama was right! He *is* crazy!
17 OLD WOMAN: Be gone! *(CORA and BITTY, tossing on*
18   *their new hats, exit Right haughtily.)* I am sorry they
19   spoke to you so, Abel.
20 ABEL: I don't think they ever understood me.
21 OLD WOMAN: I don't see how they could.
22 ABEL: But what will I do now? I'll be all alone.
23 OLD WOMAN: Not necessarily.
24   *(MERMAID holds out her hand. ABEL, slowly, happily*
25   *takes it as the curtain falls.)*

A Very Cold Case

Synopsis:
Can world-famous detective Reggie Rathbone solve a case that's fifteen years old? He's gathered all the suspects around his dining room table in hopes that he might serve up some just desserts.

Characters (4 male, 6 female):
INSPECTOR DREGG, a policeman
HETTIE HARDCOURT, a former cook
CORNELIA LINDEL, a kidnap victim
URIAH KEESH, the caterer
ABIGAIL WIMBERLY, the former nanny
LETICIA KEESH, Uriah's wife and partner
MR. TROWEL, the former gardener
MISS CRISP, Reggie Rathbone's secretary
REGGIE RATHBONE, world-famous detective
CHLOE KEESH, the caterers' niece

Setting:
The dining room of Rathbone Manor. A long banquet table covered with a cloth, set for dessert after a sumptuous feast. Small service table at Right set with punch bowl and glasses. The Upstage wall is not decorated, but hooks hang on the wall ready for use later. Chair at head of the table, Left, is empty. Entrance Down Right leads to the kitchen, Down Left to other parts of the manor. Necessarily the guests sit on the Upstage side of the table but are free to adjust their seating and movement in addition to what the stage directions require.

Props:
Coffeepot; six pieces of pie (or other dessert) on plates with forks, one for each guest; framed personal check; poster with picture of two girls, one six years old, the other about two and a half; two candy dishes holding mints; poster showing enlarged scrap of paper with "nd b" on one line, "en for 2" on a second line; punchbowl with ten cups; poster showing enlarged scrap of paper with "and bake" on one line, "in hot oven for 20 minutes" on a second line; gun; handcuffs.

Costumes:
Modern dress for all. Reggie wears smoking jacket. Leticia and Chloe wear aprons.

1	**Scene One**
2	
3	*(AT RISE: DREGG, ABIGAIL, HETTIE, TROWEL,*
4	*CORNELIA, and MISS CRISP sit at the table.*
5	*LETICIA pours coffee as URIAH serves pie or*
6	*something else for dessert to each guest.)*
7	**DREGG:** *(Annoyed, checking his watch)* **Typical!**
8	**Rathbone will be late for his own funeral!**
9	**HETTIE: Invitin' us all like this, then not showin' up**
10	**for dinner. Rude, I say! Plain rude!**
11	**CORNELIA: Well, I've certainly enjoyed dinner. It was**
12	**wonderful ... Mr. Keesh, isn't it?**
13	**URIAH: Yes, Ma'am. And my wife here and I thank**
14	**you.**
15	**HETTIE: You got some real height on your soufflé.**
16	**You do all the cooking yourselves?**
17	**LETICIA: Of course! We've been catering dinners for**
18	**many, many years.**
19	**CORNELIA: You wouldn't want to give away any of**
20	**your secret recipes, would you?**
21	**TROWEL: Wouldn't mind my missus bakin' me some of**
22	**this pie once in awhile!**
23	**LETICIA:** *(To ABIGAIL)* **Coffee, Ma'am?**
24	**ABIGAIL:** *(Frustrated)* **No! I just want to know what's**
25	**going on!**
26	**LETICIA: I'm sure I don't know, Ma'am.** *(LETICIA exits*
27	*Right with URIAH.)*
28	**MS. CRISP: Please, Ms. Wimberly, Mr. Rathbone will**
29	**be here soon.**
30	**DREGG: He missed the whole dinner, for cryin' out**
31	**loud!**
32	**MS. CRISP: As always, Mr. Rathbone has his reasons.**
33	**ABIGAIL: I didn't like the invitation in the first place**
34	**... the way it read ...** *(Mimicking)* **"Your presence**
35	**is commanded at Rathbone Manor." Like we had**

1   to come!

2   CORNELIA: What an honor, though, to be invited to

3   the home of the most famous detective in the

4   world!

5   *(REGGIE, relaxed in a smoking jacket, enters Left.)*

6   REGGIE: I thank you, Ms. Lindel. And I am so glad

7   you all could make it.

8   DREGG: 'Bout time, Rathbone!

9   REGGIE: Ah, Detective Dregg ... it has been awhile!

10   DREGG: Well, you went 'n' retired, not me!

11   TROWEL: Found enough to keep you busy, Mr.

12   Rathbone?

13   REGGIE: Oh, yes, Mr. Trowel. I have been ... tying up

14   loose ends, you might say.

15   *(ALL glance nervously at one another.)*

16   ABIGAIL: But why did you demand we come here

17   tonight?

18   HETTIE: Not that the dinner wasn't good! The salmon

19   was flaky as a spring snowfall!

20   REGGIE: You are here at my request to wrap up a bit

21   of business which began fifteen years ago.

22   DREGG: What business is that?

23   REGGIE: You should all know, of course. Ms. Crisp?

24   *(MS. CRISP stands and holds up a check in a frame.)*

25   Ms. Crisp holds up a check which I have taken

26   the precaution to frame.

27   MS. CRISP: The check is made out to Mr. Rathbone

28   for the sum of eighty thousand dollars.

29   *(ALL gasp.)*

30   REGGIE: A sizable amount of money, no?

31   HETTIE: I wouldn't have framed it! I'd have cashed

32   that faster than an egg can poach!

33   REGGIE: Never!

34   ABIGAIL: But why not?

35   REGGIE: It was paid following a case I worked

1   ceaselessly on ... but unfortunately was unable to
2   solve. *(A beat)* Until now.
3   *(Again, suspicious glances all around.)*
4   CORNELIA: Who ... who is the check from, Mr.
5   Rathbone?
6   REGGIE: It is signed, "Charles Frasher."
7   *(CORNELIA drops her fork.)*
8   ABIGAIL: Oh, I knew it had to be something like this
9   ... after all, all of us together again ... after so
10   many years.
11   DREGG: I was afraid this little gathering would have
12   something to do with all that!
13   HETTIE: We were asked so many questions right after
14   it happened, I don't think I can take another ...
15   not even fifteen years later.
16   ABIGAIL: *(Thinking back, sadly)* Those poor little
17   girls ...
18   TROWEL: At least one of 'em was spared.
19   HETTIE: A body wonders whatever became of her.
20   REGGIE: Why, she is sitting at this very table.
21   *(REGGIE moves behind CORNELIA.)* Allow me to
22   introduce you to Jenny Frasher, who is now
23   Cornelia Lindel.
24   ABIGAIL: *(Shocked)* You! You're ... you're little ...
25   Jenny?
26   TROWEL: I don't believe it!
27   HETTIE: *(Suspiciously)* Let's get a look at you!
28   MS. CRISP: Oh, there's no doubt about it. This is
29   Jenny Frasher.
30   CORNELIA: And I do remember all of you. Mr.
31   Rathbone asked me not to say anything until he
32   introduced me. I hope you don't think I've been
33   rude.
34   ABIGAIL: But, you've changed so!
35   CORNELIA: Mother and father made sure of that ...

1   even to changing my name. But, Mr. Rathbone,
2   you said you've solved the case. Does it really
3   matter now? I mean ... my poor little sister has
4   been gone so long ...
5 REGGIE: It most certainly makes a difference, Ms.
6   Lindel. After all, justice, like dessert, must be
7   served!
8 DREGG: And after fifteen years *you* solved this thing?
9   C'mon, Rathbone! Even for a man of your talents,
10   that's hard to believe.
11 REGGIE: As is so often the case, a memory linked
12   with a chance encounter has produced
13   unfavorable results for the criminal.
14 ABIGAIL: Who *is* the criminal, then, Mr. Rathbone?
15 REGGIE: I can assure you, the perpetrator is here, as
16   we speak.
17 DREGG: Then out with it! *(Rising)* None of us has time
18   for your usual theatrics!
19 REGGIE: Sit down, Inspector ... and now that you
20   have enjoyed your dessert, let us serve the just
21   desserts. Ms. Crisp? *(REGGIE sits at head of table as*
22   *MS. CRISP stands.)*
23 MS. CRISP: Fifteen years ago this very night, two
24   little girls were kidnapped from their bedroom at
25   Frasher House. *(MS. CRISP holds up poster size*
26   *photo of two young girls, about six and two in age.)*
27   Jenny was six, while her sister Jessica was two.
28   *(MS. CRISP hangs the poster on one of the hooks on*
29   *the Upstage wall.)*
30 CORNELIA: Oh, Jessica!
31 ABIGAIL: Poor little thing!
32 TROWEL: *(Smiling at the memory)* How she loved to
33   chase butterflies in the garden!
34 HETTIE: She even helped me dry dishes. Plastic ones,
35   of course.

1   MS. CRISP: A telephone call to Charles Frasher
2   demanded a ransom of a hundred thousand
3   dollars. Mr. Frasher did exactly as he was told
4   and followed instructions for the drop even to the
5   point of delivering the money alone. However,
6   neither girl was delivered the next day to Frasher
7   House as promised.
8   REGGIE: *(Angrily)* Nor the next day ... nor the next ...
9   nor the next! Tell us what happened, Ms. Lindel.
10   CORNELIA: *(Rising)* Must I?
11   HETTIE: You poor dear! I wouldn't say a thing.
12   REGGIE: But it is almost over, Ms. Lindel. Tell us how
13   you escaped.
14   CORNELIA: It was horrible. They kept us in a small
15   barn or shed or something like that. I can't really
16   say because they tied bags of fabric over our
17   heads. And they'd taped our hands and feet with
18   duct tape. But I could smell the hay and there
19   was a goat. He was our only friend ... and he had
20   a taste for tape. He liked to chew it.
21   DREGG: They like the glue, don't they?
22   CORNELIA: That's right. And as he chewed, my
23   hands got free ... and then my legs. I was trying
24   to untape the bag over my head when I heard
25   someone coming. I knew I had to get out, so I
26   kissed Jessica and promised her I'd come back
27   for her. I promised ... but all I remember now is
28   her crying ... and crying ... as I stumbled out of
29   that place.
30   REGGIE: *(Gently)* And then you wandered blindly
31   through the woods.
32   CORNELIA: Yes ... walking into trees, tripping over
33   branches, all the while struggling with the bag on
34   my head. Suddenly I walked onto pavement, and
35   I saw lights through the bag and heard the

1   screech of brakes.

2 MS. CRSIP: A motorist fortunately swerved, stopped

3   his car, and took you immediately to safety.

4 CORNELIA: *(Sitting)* Yes ... but Jessie ... poor Jessie

5   ... was never found.

6 MS. CRISP: By the time the police found the shack,

7   the kidnapper had cleared out ... with your sister.

8 REGGIE: He ... or she ... had been careful enough to

9   remove every clue ... except for one that was

10   found in the pocket of your sweater.

11 DREGG: You were dressed in old clothes ... odds and

12   ends the kidnapper had ... and your nightclothes

13   must have been destroyed.

14 CORNELIA: I suppose so. But I never knew there was

15   anything in the pocket, Mr. Rathbone.

16 DREGG: Kept that a secret, we did. Can't let

17   everything out to the press!

18 HETTIE: *(Suspiciously)* What was it?

19 ABIGAIL: And what does it mean to us? *(URIAH and*

20   *LETICIA enter Right carrying candy dishes.)*

21 URIAH: Begging your pardon, but we've brought

22   after-dinner mints.

23 LETICIA: Homemade, I might add.

24 REGGIE: Excellent! Feel free to serve them, and then,

25   please stay because we'll need you to serve the

26   punch.

27   *(URIAH bows, and discreetly he and LETICIA serve*

28   *mints and perhaps more coffee.)*

29 TROWEL: *(To REGGIE)* You sure don't think any of us

30   had anything to do with the crime!

31 ABIGAIL: *(Rising)* I know I had nothing to do with

32   such a horrible thing! I'm leaving! I don't want to

33   hear any more of this! I heard enough fifteen

34   years ago! *(ABIGAIL exits Left angrily.)*

35 DREGG: Want me to stop her, Rathbone?

1   REGGIE: No need, Detective. *(HETTIE rises angrily and*
2   *moves Right.)* **You have need of the restroom, Ms.**
3   **Hardcourt?**
4   HETTIE: I ... I don't feel well ... I need some air.
5   REGGIE: Please, go through the kitchen, then, into
6   the garden. It sparkles at night with the fragrance
7   of lilacs and roses. *(HETTIE exits Right.)*
8   DREGG: But if either of them's the one —
9   REGGIE: Oh, they'll be back ... and in the meantime
10   I can proceed with the only clue found in the
11   entire case. It was a small piece of paper ... very
12   common paper ... and on it was written a
13   smattering of letters. It looked like this: *(MS.*
14   *CRISP holds up a poster. It shows an enlargement of*
15   *a scrap of paper on which we see the letters "nd b" on*
16   *a top row and "en for 2" on a second row. She hangs*
17   *poster on the Upstage wall.)*
18   MS. CRISP: The interesting thing is that while the
19   letters are of an almost print-like quality, they are
20   handwritten.
21   REGGIE: Fifteen years ago, each of you was asked to
22   write something in your own hand and each
23   sample was balanced against the writing here.
24   But there was no match. Still — *(ABIGAIL enters*
25   *Left.)*
26   ABIGAIL: My car won't start! I just had it serviced,
27   and it's dead!
28   REGGIE: *(Calmly)* Such a pity.
29   ABIGAIL: Detective, I demand you take me to town
30   where I can catch a bus!
31   REGGIE: But I'm afraid the detective's car won't start,
32   either.
33   DREGG: What?
34   MS. CRISP: During dinner, Mr. Rathbone took the
35   liberty of ensuring your full cooperation,

1   Detective Dregg.

2   TROWEL: Here, now! There's laws against stuff like

3   that!

4   REGGIE: We   have   not   permanently   damaged

5   anything.

6   ABIGAIL: But I want to leave!

7   REGGIE: And you shall, soon enough. If you would be

8   so good as to rejoin us? *(HETTIE enters Right.)* **Ah,**

9   the faithful cook returns.

10   HETTIE: *(Angrily, glancing Right)* I've never been so

11   insulted in my life!

12   REGGIE: What is it, Ms. Hardcourt?

13   HETTIE: That dishwasher they got in there accused

14   *me* of makin' a mess on her clean floor!

15   LETICIA: Oh, we're sorry, Ma'am. She's our niece

16   Chloe, 'n' she's very headstrong.

17   URIAH: I'll go have a talkin' to her right now.

18   REGGIE: Quite unnecessary, Mr. Keesh. If we don't

19   disturb her, she'll be able to get her work done.

20   And so, where was I?

21   CORNELIA: The clue. That bit of paper in my pocket.

22   REGGIE: Ah, yes! We studied it and studied it ... but

23   it made no sense.

24   DREGG: Had to be a code of some kind.

25   ABIGAIL: None of us knows anything about it.

26   TROWEL: That's right. Nobody discussed clues with us

27   suspects, that's for sure!

28   REGGIE: *(Moving to ABIGAIL)* You were the girls'

29   nanny, were you not, Ms. Wimberly?

30   ABIGAIL: Yes, but ...

31   REGGIE: And you were in the room next to theirs?

32   ABIGAIL: I told the police ... I told everyone ... I'd

33   taken a sleeping pill because I'd had trouble

34   sleeping! I never heard a thing! Not a thing!

35   REGGIE: You needed money at the time, didn't you?

1   Your trouble with sleeping was caused by the fact
2   your brother had been arrested, and you needed
3   to find some way to put up his bail and find him
4   a lawyer?
5 ABIGAIL: But I wouldn't have hurt Jenny or Jessica
6   for the likes of him!
7 REGGIE: Perhaps not. Ms. Hardcourt, just after the
8   kidnapping your husband died, is that correct?
9 HETTIE: You know all about it.
10 REGGIE: He had been sick for quite some time. He
11   had good insurance, but the benefits were eaten
12   up by his long illness as were your personal
13   savings. Thus you had to continue working as a
14   cook all these years.
15 HETTIE: *(With injured dignity)* Nothin' wrong with
16   good, hard work, Mr. Rathbone!
17 DREGG: Really, Rathbone!
18 REGGIE: *(Ignoring him)* And that night, Ms.
19   Hardcourt, you were in your room with your
20   husband, weren't you?
21 HETTIE: Yes, and just like I told the police, all I
22   heard was a truck driving away.
23 REGGIE: Precisely at nine p.m.
24 HETTIE: Yes! I'd just given my poor Billy his evening
25   dose of painkiller.
26 REGGIE: And you're sure it was a truck?
27 HETTIE: A small truck, yes. Not one of those semis,
28   but a small one.
29 TROWEL: But I never heard a thing!
30 MS. CRISP: From the gardener's house, it would have
31   been difficult.
32 REGGIE: Especially for someone hard of hearing.
33   Unless, of course ...
34 TROWEL: *(Offended)* Unless what?
35 REGGIE: Unless someone knew it was a truck, but

1   didn't want to verify that fact for some reason.

2   TROWEL: *(Angrily)* Now, look here, Mr. Rathbone!

3   REGGIE: Again, money would have come in handy at

4   that time, would it not, Mr. Trowel?

5   TROWEL: When wouldn't it come in handy?

6   REGGIE: You had the opportunity at that time for a

7   partnership in a gardening supply store, isn't that

8   right?

9   TROWEL: But I didn't get it, did I? If I'd had a

10   hundred   thousand   dollars,   I'd   have   done

11   everything I wanted!

12   REGGIE: A very good point, Mr. Trowel.

13   DREGG: *(Tiredly)* We've been over and over all this,

14   Rathbone.

15   REGGIE: And you, Detective Dregg, my good friend.

16   Not solving this case cost you a promotion, didn't

17   it?

18   DREGG: I wasn't the first person ever overlooked. I

19   won't be the last, either.

20   REGGIE: You see my point? You have all suffered. Far

21   more than I! Not one of you appears to have

22   gained a thing by what happened that night. Yet

23   the weight of suspicion hangs very heavily on

24   your shoulders ... even now, fifteen years later. I

25   wish at this time to propose a toast!

26   DREGG: *(Incredulously)* A toast?!

27   *(REGGIE moves to punchbowl.)*

28   REGGIE: Humor me, Detective. *(REGGIE has his back*

29   *to audience, but it is clear he is tampering with the*

30   *glasses.)* Mr. Keesh? Mrs. Keesh? *(URIAH bows, and*

31   *he and LETICIA serve the glasses REGGIE fills very*

32   *carefully, his back still to the audience.)* A toast is

33   good for the soul. It will help us remember those

34   days — those happier days before this terrible

35   tragedy. And it will help us to realize that we may

1   **soon return to the happiness we once cherished.**
2   *(ALL guests have glasses by now.)* **And you, Mr. and**
3   **Mrs. Keesh ...** *(He holds out a glass for each of them.)*
4 URIAH: **Oh, sir, we couldn't ...**
5 REGGIE: **Perhaps, then, in honor of the splendid**
6   **dinner you served!**
7 LETICIA: *(Flattered)* **Well, in** *that* **case!** *(She takes glass*
8   *from REGGIE, who then gives the other to URIAH.*
9   *REGGIE picks up a glass for himself.)*
10 REGGIE: **And now, we hold our glasses high to the**
11   **two Frasher girls and to the happiness they**
12   **shared!** *(ALL drink.)* **And further, may they soon**
13   **share the happiness they missed all these years.**
14   *(ABIGAIL drops her glass.)*
15 ABIGAIL: **Oh, dear!**
16 HETTIE: **Now see what you've done, Mr. Know It All!**
17 CORNELIA: *(To REGGIE)* **How can you say something**
18   **so cruel?**
19 REGGIE: **Because it's true!**
20 DREGG: **Jessica Frasher's dead, Rathbone! She's been**
21   **dead for the past fifteen years!**
22 REGGIE: **But no trace was ever found.**
23 DREGG: **Nothing, but that doesn't mean —**
24 REGGIE: **Isn't that, in itself, suspicious?**
25 CORNELIA: **Please, Mr. Rathbone ...**
26 REGGIE: **I do not wish to be cruel, Ms. Lindel. Soon**
27   **you will see the light of dawn.** *(MS. CRISP coughs.)*
28   **Everything all right, Ms. Crisp?**
29 MS. CRISP: **Oh, I'm just fine, Mr. Rathbone.**
30 REGGIE: **You look a bit pale.**
31 MS. CRISP: **No, really ... I'm fine.**
32 REGGIE: **You can't be too careful ... especially after**
33   **that nasty bout with pneumonia several weeks**
34   **ago.**
35 DREGG: **Rathbone! We're sorry to hear about your**

1   secretary's illness, but this is getting us nowhere!
2 REGGIE: Ms. Crisp's pneumonia will get us
3   everywhere.
4 HETTIE: I think he's flipped like a pancake!
5 TROWEL: Detective, you're a policeman! Do
6   something!
7 DREGG: You're trying my patience, Rathbone!
8 REGGIE: Then let us move swiftly.
9 URIAH: Sir, if you don't mind, we'd like to get back
10   'n' help Chloe with the cleaning.
11 LETICIA: We've got to get home so we can work on
12   tomorrow's party. We're serving at the Gladstones.
13   Engagement party, it is.
14 REGGIE: Ah, the traveling life of the caterers.
15 URIAH: Been good to us all these years.
16 REGGIE: Please do me one last favor. Serve a bit
17   more punch, and then you are dismissed. *(URIAH*
18   *bows, and he and LETICIA serve more punch.)* **Now,**
19   back to Ms. Crisp's pneumonia. It was a serious
20   case, was it not?
21 MS. CRISP: I spent a week in the hospital.
22 REGGIE: Which means you were not here.
23 DREGG: *(Sarcastically)* Good thinking, Rathbone!
24 REGGIE: And this left me to ramble all alone in this
25   great house.
26 HETTIE: We should all have to suffer so!
27 REGGIE: But you wouldn't. You see, you all have very
28   practical skills. You, Ms. Hardcourt, can cook.
29   You, Ms. Wimberly, can raise and educate
30   children. You, Detective Dregg, can find and
31   arrest the criminal. And you, Mr. Trowel, can
32   grow a garden. Even the Keeshes can prepare and
33   serve a feast. I can do none of these things. All I
34   can do is think. But what good is that when one
35   is hungry? And I did get hungry.

1 DREGG: The point, Rathbone?
2 REGGIE: The point, Detective, is that I got hungry for
3   food not out of crinkly bags. So I decided to try
4   my hand at cooking.
5 HETTIE: Well, bully for you!
6 REGGIE: I took a cookbook off the shelf. I decided I
7   had a yen for a raspberry tart. And so I found a
8   recipe. And I began to assemble flour, butter,
9   sugar ... and then I stopped.
10 ABIGIAL: Why?
11 REGGIE: That is when I realized!
12 TROWEL: Realized what?
13 REGGIE: What was on the scrap of paper found in the
14   pocket of the sweater Ms. Lindel was wearing so
15   very long ago. Ms. Crisp?
16 *(MS. CRISP hangs a third poster, this one showing*
17 *part of a recipe, which includes the exact letters on the*
18 *second poster: "and bake in a hot oven for 20*
19 *minutes.")*
20 TROWEL: What are you getting at?
21 REGGIE: The old sweater you wore, Ms. Lindel ...
22   belonged to one of the kidnappers. And this
23   person had left a bit of a recipe behind.
24 DREGG: A recipe! You mean this kidnapper might
25   have been the — *(DREGG looks at HETTIE*
26   *suspiciously.)*
27 HETTIE: Now, see here!
28 REGGIE: The person who kidnapped the Frasher girls
29   should already be starting to feel very dizzy. For
30   I have put a bit of justice in the punch you were
31   given. After all, it must be served somehow. Soon
32   you will fall into a sleep ... and then ... mercifully
33   ... the poison will take full effect.
34 ABIGAIL: *(Terrified)* Poison?!
35 REGGIE: We all want to see the guilty punished.

1 DREGG: But ... but that's taking the law into your
2   own hands, Rathbone!
3 REGGIE: I am prepared to suffer the consequences,
4   Detective! *(ALL look one to another. HETTIE rises, as*
5   *if to leave again, but halts.)* Perhaps you feel faint,
6   Ms. Hardcourt? Or you, Mr. Trowel?
7 TROWEL: *(Terrified)* No! No!
8 CORNELIA: Who is it? Stop this nonsense now!
9   *(LETICIA faints.)*
10 DREGG: Mrs. Keesh!
11 REGGIE: *(As DREGG and URIAH kneel by her)* Yes, Mrs.
12   Keesh. Yes ... it had to be someone who cooked.
13   But this is not really Mrs. Keesh at all.
14 URIAH: She's ... she's just a bit ... overworked! I don't
15   know what you're talking about!
16 ABIGAIL: Do something, Mr. Rathbone! She's going to
17   die!
18 REGGIE: There wasn't any poison, Ms. Wimberly. It
19   was nothing but a mixture of the power of
20   suggestion along with guilt. You see, it was Mr.
21   Keesh and his sister here, then known as Jake
22   and Myra Ferris who kidnapped the children
23   fifteen years ago.
24 URIAH: That's a lie!
25 REGGIE: No, Mr. Keesh. Ferris Catering served a
26   dinner at the Frasher house three days before the
27   kidnapping. You desperately needed money to
28   cover a gambling debt. While serving the dinner
29   you must have hatched the scheme.
30 URIAH: I don't know any Jake Ferris! Nobody saw me
31   at that house!
32 REGGIE: Mrs. Frasher described the caterers as a
33   man with a short, dark beard, glasses, and a small
34   scar on his forehead. The woman was blonde with
35   blue eyes. Very simple to change your

1   appearance. You used that dinner to get the
2   layout of the house.
3 URIAH: You can't prove anything!
4 REGGIE: The truck Ms. Hardcourt heard was the
5   Ferris catering truck, an old one you got rid of
6   after you had the close call at the shack where
7   you hid the girls. I have a copy of the bill of sale.
8   The salesman had the foresight to retain a
9   photocopy of your licenses which bear your
10   pictures. You with your dark beard, glasses, and
11   scar. And the police have already taken your
12   personal papers. Among them will we find the
13   torn recipe missing just this final bit of
14   information?
15   *(URIAH pulls out a gun.)*
16 URIAH: Clever, Rathbone! Real clever! But we got
17   away with it once, and we'll do it again! *(Calling*
18   *Right)* Chloe! Get the truck started!
19 DREGG: *(To URIAH)* You can't get away with this!
20 CORNELIA: *(To URIAH)* It was you! That shout! I
21   heard you shout like that often!
22 REGGIE: And when you were describing being
23   hidden in the shack, Ms. Lindel, you said "they."
24   You knew instinctively there were at least two of
25   them.
26 TROWEL: He'd have to have someone to shout at,
27   wouldn't he?
28 URIAH: *(To LETICIA)* Get up, you lazy thing! I'm not
29   doin' all the work! Get up! Chloe! Get the truck
30   started, hear me?
31 ABIGAIL: What are you going to do with us?
32 URIAH: Chloe! *(DREGG grabs URIAH's arm, and there's*
33   *a brief struggle. The gun can go off for dramatic*
34   *effect if desired. DREGG is knocked to the floor.)*
35   Now, all of you! Back over there!

1   *(LETICIA rises as others crowd to Down Left corner.)*
2   LETICIA: You fool! Now they know!
3   URIAH: He figured it out, don't kid yourself! And
4   there's no poison in that stuff you drank!
5   LETICIA: For crying out loud!
6   URIAH: I told you we shouldn't have taken this job!
7   LETICIA: He offered us twice our usual! With your
8   debts we couldn't afford to turn it down! So
9   what'll we do with 'em?
10   *(CHLOE, a slovenly girl of seventeen, enters Right.)*
11   CHLOE: What're you shouting at me for?
12   URIAH: Here! Hold this on 'em! Any of 'em move,
13   shoot! *(URIAH shoves the gun into CHLOE's hands.)*
14   CHLOE: *(Incredulously)* What?
15   URIAH: Leticia! Get some rope! Tape, too!
16   LETICIA: What are we going to do?
17   URIAH: Do like I say, and ask questions later!
18   REGGIE: *(To CHLOE)* Ms. Keesh, we enjoyed dinner
19   very much.
20   CHLOE: What's all this about?
21   REGGIE: Do you remember any of these people?
22   URIAH: Shoot him!
23   REGGIE: Look at the guests, especially at Ms. Lindel
24   here.
25   *(CORNELIA steps forward.)*
26   CHLOE: That's far enough!
27   REGGIE: Say something, Ms. Lindel!
28   CORNELIA: Mr. Rathbone, what am I supposed to —
29   CHLOE: *(Thinking, nervously)* I know you! Why do I
30   know you?
31   URIAH: You don't know any of 'em, stupid girl!
32   CHLOE: *(Noticing first poster on wall)* Who are they?
33   REGGIE: It's Ms. Lindel ... and you.
34   CORNELIA: What?
35   DREGG: Rathbone, you're crazy!

1 CHLOE: I remember a dress like that ... I think ...
2   maybe ...
3 URIAH: Give me the gun! Give it to me!
4 CHLOE: No!
5   *(REGGIE and DREGG rush to URIAH and grapple*
6   *him to the floor. DREGG handcuffs URIAH.)*
7 URIAH: Stupid girl! Stupid girl! You should have shot
8   'em!
9 DREGG: Come with me, Mr. Keesh! You've got a lot of
10   questions to answer!
11 REGGIE: Be sure to pick up Mrs. Keesh on your way
12   out, Detective. I'm sure she ran off to the truck,
13   but it won't go very far. And, Detective, perhaps
14   now you'll get that promotion. *(DREGG pushes*
15   *URIAH Off Right. REGGIE gently takes gun from*
16   *CHLOE who stares at the picture.)* Keesh didn't want
17   to keep either of you, but his sister wouldn't give
18   you up, Chloe. She most likely threatened to go to
19   the police if he tried to warn you ... or worse.
20 CHLOE: I'm their niece ...
21 REGGIE: It's what they wanted you to believe.
22 CORNELIA: Jessie?
23 CHLOE: *(Thinking back)* Jessie?
24 ABIGAIL: Oh, dear me! Can it really be you?
25 REGGIE: The Keeshes held you all these years.
26 CHLOE: *(Confused and angry)* No! They're my aunt and
27   uncle. They took me in when my parents died in
28   a plane crash.
29 HETTIE: They must have invented that story, dear.
30   You never had an aunt or uncle.
31 CHLOE: Then I'm alone. I've got no one but them!
32 CORNELIA: No, no, no! You've got a family who's
33   never before been this happy. I'm your sister,
34   Jenny. I'm the other girl in the picture.
35 CHLOE: My sister?

81

1   *(CORNELIA nods, embraces CHLOE.)*
2   **REGGIE: And now to the real purpose of our dinner**
3   **... a reunion. A long-overdue reunion!** *(As others*
4   *talk animatedly with CHLOE and one another,*
5   *REGGIE and MS. CRISP move Down Right with*
6   *punch glasses.)* **Ah, it is good to serve up justice,**
7   **don't you think, Ms. Crisp?**
8   *(They clink their glasses as the curtain falls.)*

Mystery of the Magical Forest

Synopsis:
What strange secret does the Magical Forest hold? Hopeful gardener Leo must find out or lose his hope of finding his fortune in the city just beyond.

Characters (3 male, 2 female, 1 male or female):
LEO, a young gardener
GERTRUDE, a baker
TROLL (male or female)
SIGMUND, the magician's assistant
NONA, the magician's daughter
MILBURN, the magician

Props:
Basket covered with cloth; shiny new shovel; backpack for Leo; watering can; 10 tulip (or other) bulbs; treasure chest containing gold objects such as candlesticks, gold coins (at least 10), frames, statues, etc; suitcase.
Note: Have extra flowers with which to fill the flowerpots and decorate the garden for the last scene of the play.

Costumes:
Any style desired. Sigmund and Nona each need a long gray or navy cape which can turn into the "rock" formation as mentioned in the script.

1	**Scene One**
2	
3	*A path through the Magical Forest, played before the*
4	*curtain. "Rock" at center (figure covered in gray fabric).*
5	*(AT RISE: GERTRUDE enters Right, nervously*
6	*looking back. She holds basket covered with cloth. LEO*
7	*enters Left carrying shovel. He watches GERTRUDE*
8	*with amusement. She backs into LEO and screams.)*
9	LEO: **I'm sorry! I didn't mean to frighten you!**
10	GERTRUDE: **Well, I'm glad it's only you. I was afraid**
11	**it was ... him!**
12	LEO: **Him?**
13	GERTRUDE: **You're not from around here, are you?**
14	LEO: **No. I'm Leo, the gardener. I have ten gold coins,**
15	**ten tulip bulbs, and my shiny new shovel. I am on**
16	**my way to the city to make my fortune.**
17	GERTRUDE: **But to get to the city, you must walk**
18	**through this forest. The Magical Forest!**
19	LEO: **I have walked through dark and gloomy forests**
20	**before!**
21	GERTRUDE: **But this one is special. It is guarded by a**
22	**Troll who can smell gold. You must give him all**
23	**your coins, or he will turn you into a rock. Do you**
24	**see all those rocks?** *(GERTRUDE points into*
25	*audience. LEO looks at audience and nods.)* **All of**
26	**those are people just like you who couldn't get**
27	**past the Troll.**
28	LEO: **What does the Troll want with gold?**
29	GERTRUDE: **It's for the magician's daughter, Nona.**
30	**She's the greediest person alive. The only way**
31	**Milburn the Magician can get her everything she**
32	**wants for keeping her happy is to rob poor**
33	**travelers.**
34	LEO: *(Jovially)* **What a silly story!**
35	GERTRUDE: **Take heed, sir! There is only one way to**

1   sneak past the Troll.
2   LEO: *(Laughing)* What is this way?
3   GERTRUDE: The Troll loves cream puffs more than
4   gold. Have you a cream puff on you?
5   LEO: Me? I don't need a cream puff!
6   GERTRUDE: I would give you one, but I gave all I had
7   to the Troll, so now my fortune is safe.
8   LEO: If I see this Troll, I'll box his ears!
9   *(GERTRUDE moves Left with her basket.)*
10   GERTRUDE: I see there's no use in warning you, sir.
11   You must learn the hard way. Good day. And good
12   luck. *(GERTRUDE exits Left. LEO puffs out his chest*
13   *and exits Right. A moment later, he backs on as TROLL*
14   *enters Right. TROLL is fearful looking.)*
15   LEO: *(Terrified)* You ... you ... you don't scare me,
16   Troll. Sir. Madam. Whatever.
17   TROLL: Fee fie fool fold ... I smell a bag of gold!
18   LEO: I ... I have no gold!
19   TROLL: Give me your gold!
20   LEO: Never!
21   TROLL: Very well, I will have to spin it from you.
22   *(TROLL makes circular motion with his hand, and*
23   *LEO begins to spin around.)*
24   LEO: *(Spinning)* Wait! What's happening? What are you
25   doing to me? Help! Help! *(LEO drops gold from his*
26   *belt. TROLL picks it up as LEO continues to spin. Once*
27   *TROLL has the gold, he puts up his hand, and LEO*
28   *stops spinning.)*
29   TROLL: Thank you, sir!
30   LEO: But that's all the money I have. Please, Sir ...
31   Madam ... Whatever.
32   TROLL: It's not much, but it's something. *(TROLL exits*
33   *Right. LEO sits on "rock.")*
34   LEO: Now what'll I do? My ten gold pieces are gone! *(He*
35   *begins to cry loudly. He blows his nose. The rock begins*

1   *to move. LEO jumps up.)* **Hey! What's going on?**
2   *(SIGMUND rises. It was his gray cloak that had formed*
3   *the rock.)*
4   **SIGMUND:** *(Stretching)* **Why, thank you, sir!**
5   **LEO: You're a rock!**
6   **SIGMUND: No longer, thanks to you. Your tears broke**
7   **the spell. The Troll can turn anyone he wants to**
8   **into a rock, and the spell can only be broken by**
9   **human tears.**
10 **LEO: If you don't mind my saying, this is one weird**
11 **forest!**
12 **SIGMUND: That's why it's called the Magical Forest.**
13 **Allow me to introduce myself. I am Sigmund,**
14 **assistant to Milburn the Magician.**
15 **LEO: Oh, so this is all your fault!**
16 **SIGMUND: Not really. I've been a rock ever since I**
17 **tried to stop the Troll. I found out what Milburn**
18 **was doing and wanted to undo it, but my power**
19 **wasn't great enough. The Troll must have robbed**
20 **you, too, huh?**
21 **LEO: I'm Leo the gardener. I came with ten gold coins,**
22 **ten tulip bulbs, and my shiny new shovel to make**
23 **my fortune in the city. But now all my money's**
24 **gone.**
25 **SIGMUND: Your story sounds familiar. Tell me ...**
26 **would you be interested in getting your money**
27 **back?**
28 **LEO: I'll say!**
29 **SIGMUND: It will be dangerous ... but we must do**
30 **something. This forest was once beautiful. But**
31 **ever since Milburn's daughter became so greedy, it**
32 **has withered like everything else.**
33 **LEO: What can we do about it?**
34 **SIGMUND:** *(Moving Left, looking carefully)* **We must sneak**
35 **into Milburn's castle! Come along!** *(SIGMUND leads*

1   *LEO Off Right quickly as lights Dim.)*
2
3   **Scene Two**
4
5   *That night, in the garden of Milburn's castle. At Center*
6   *is a large flowerpot which has one pretty flower and a*
7   *few dead weeds sprouting from it. Down Right and Left*
8   *are two smaller pots filled the same way. A garden*
9   *bench Right Center. A leafless tree Left. Water can sits*
10   *by flowerpot, Center.*
11   *(AT RISE: NONA stands shouting Off Left.)*
12 NONA: *(Furiously)* You're fired, and you're never to
13   come back here!
14   *(MILBURN enters Right.)*
15 MILBURN: Nona, my lovely daughter, where are all
16   the servants?
17 NONA: *(Pouting)* I threw them all out.
18 MILBURN: The cook?
19 NONA: She wouldn't give me enough candy!
20 MILBURN: The coachman?
21 NONA: He wouldn't let me take the coach by myself.
22 MILBURN: The gardener?
23 NONA: He wouldn't let me wear this flower in my hair!
24 MILBURN: *(Painfully)* But that's the last living thing in
25   this garden.
26   *(NONA plucks the flower and puts it in her hair.)*
27 NONA: Oh, daddy ... just open up your book of spells
28   and wave your magic wand, and we can have
29   anything we want.
30 MILBURN: I cannot do magic anymore, my darling.
31 NONA: What?
32 MILBURN: I cannot concentrate on anything!
33 NONA: You'd better start concentrating because I
34   want a boyfriend!
35 MILBURN: Nona, perhaps it's time you learned that

1 we can't have everything we want in life.
2 NONA: I can!
3 MILBURN: Since your mother died, I have tried to be
4 a good father and give you whatever your heart
5 desires. But all you want is more and more! The
6 forest is dead ... the people grumble because their
7 gold is stolen ... our house is empty of happiness,
8 and nothing grows in the garden anymore.
9 NONA: So?
10 MILBURN: No one will work for us anymore ... and as
11 for a boyfriend ... even magic won't help you find
12 one of those!
13 NONA: *(Stomping her foot)* I don't want to find one on
14 my own! I want you to get me one! And I want a
15 new pair of earrings and a new dress to wear! And
16 if you don't get them, I'll hold my breath until I
17 turn blue! *(She holds her breath dramatically.)*
18 MILBURN: Please, Nona! Don't behave this way! There's
19 nothing I can do!
20 *(LEO enters Right with shovel and backpack.)*
21 LEO: Excuse me ... is this the castle of Milburn the
22 Magician?
23 MILBURN: I am Milburn, and this is my daughter,
24 Nona.
25 *(NONA gasps for a breath.)*
26 LEO: I am Leo, the gardener.
27 NONA: *(Looking him over)* You're a bit scruffy.
28 LEO: But I can work miracles in the soil. And it looks
29 like this garden needs a miracle!
30 MILBURN: We are in need of a gardener —
31 NONA: And cook, coachman, groomsman —
32 MILBRUN: Perhaps if you could show us your
33 handiwork ...
34 LEO: *(Pulling a bulb from his backpack)* Gladly! A tulip
35 bulb, Mr. Magician, sir. *(LEO shoves the bulb into the*

1   *large flowerpot.)* **And now a bit of water.** *(He picks*
2   *up water can and waters pot.)*
3 **NONA: Anybody can do that!**
4 **LEO: Just wait! Turn around!** *(MILBURN and NONA*
5   *face audience. SIGMUND enters Right. NONA begins*
6   *to turn around, so SIGMUND ducks behind pot just in*
7   *time.)* **Ah ha! No peeking!** *(NONA sticks out her*
8   *tongue at LEO and turns around, bored. SIGMUND*
9   *rises, waves his hands. A huge tulip rises in the pot.*
10   *NOTE: Have someone inside or behind the pot who can*
11   *push up the flower at the appropriate time. SIGMUND*
12   *then slips behind the leafless tree.)* **OK, turn around!**
13 **MILBURN: This is wonderful! You are indeed a**
14   **talented gardener. You must stay and bring my**
15   **garden back to life. What price do you command?**
16   *(A bell rings.)*
17 **NONA: Daddy! Daddy! He's here! I wonder how much**
18   **he brought today!** *(NONA drags a dispirited*
19   *MILBURN Off Left. SIGMUND slips out of hiding.)*
20 **SIGMUND: The Troll must be dropping off his daily**
21   **catch.**
22 **LEO: Then I shall ask for my ten coins back.**
23 **SIGMUND: What good will that do?**
24 **LEO: I can go on to the city and make my fortune.**
25 **SIGMUND: And let the Troll continue to rob innocent**
26   **people? Leave Nona to continue her greedy life?**
27 **LEO: I guess that would be terrible. But what can we**
28   **do?** *(SIGMUND whispers in LEO's ear.)* **I should?**
29   *(SIGMUND nods, then hides behind the tree. LEO*
30   *begins planting more bulbs. MILBURN enters Left*
31   *followed by NONA who carries a treasure chest.)*
32 **MILBURN: It was a very busy day in the forest.**
33 **NONA: Yeah, this is real heavy!**
34 **LEO:** *(Moving to her)* **Allow me to help you.**
35 **NONA:** *(Greedily)* **Don't touch it! It's mine! All mine!**

1   (*NONA places chest on bench and pulls from it a gold*
2   *candlestick or two, bags of coins, gold frames, whatever*
3   *— as long as it's gold.*) **Oh, Daddy, I can get that**
4   **new dress now ... and some candy ... and new**
5   **shoes!**
6   **MILBURN:** (*Disheartened*) **Whatever your little heart**
7   **desires.** (*To LEO*) **And you, sir? What does your**
8   **heart desire?**
9   **LEO: Well, sir, I know your garden is important to you.**
10   **MILBURN: I love my garden. And I don't know what**
11   **has happened to it. I want to see it beautiful again.**
12   **Name your price.**
13   **LEO: I want half of what is in the treasure chest.**
14   **MILBURN:** (*Shocked*) **Half?**
15   **NONA:** (*Angry*) **You can't have** *any* **of it!**
16   **MILBURN:** (*Gently*) **Now, Nona, dear ...**
17   **LEO: I said half, and I mean half!**
18   **MILBURN: Well, now, Nona ... you can spare half of it**
19   **today.**
20   **LEO: Half of it every day.**
21   **NONA: I** *told* **you he was no good!**
22   **MILBURN: Now, Nona, don't you want the garden to**
23   **bloom again?**
24   **NONA:** (*Furiously*) **I don't care about the stupid garden!**
25   **He can't have any of my gold!**
26   **LEO: Then good day to you ...** (*LEO walks Right.*
27   *SIGMUND, from behind tree, waves his hands. The*
28   *tulip in the center pot disappears.*)
29   **MILBURN: No, wait!** (*LEO stops.*) **I'm sure my daughter**
30   **will share with you.**
31   **NONA:** (*Pouting*) **Share? I don't share with anybody!**
32   **MILBURN: But Nona!** (*He picks up the chest.*)
33   **NONA: I'll hold my breath 'til I turn blue!** (*She does so.*
34   *MILBURN gives half the gold to LEO, who puts it in*
35   *his backpack. NONA suddenly exhales and gasps for*

1 *breath.)* **Daddy! You're not being fair! Give me my**
2 **gold back right now!**
3 MILBURN: **No!**
4 NONA: *(Gasping in fury)* **You ... you never said "no" to**
5 **me before! You ... you don't love me any more!**
6 *(NONA runs Off Left.)*
7 MILBURN: *(Carrying chest, following her Off Left)* **Nona!**
8 **Nona! I do love you!** *(He exits.)*
9 LEO: *(Calling Off Left)* **I'll start my work in the**
10 **morning, Mr. Magician, sir.**
11 *(SIGMUND comes out of hiding. He picks up backpack*
12 *and places it Center Stage.)*
13 SIGMUND: **We'll place this right here.**
14 LEO: **What are you doing?**
15 SIGMUND: **You'll see.** *(He looks up.)* **I think night is just**
16 **about to fall.** *(If possible, lights dim suddenly.*
17 *SIGMUND and LEO lie down and curl up on floor.*
18 *They go to sleep. NONA, wearing a dark cloak and*
19 *hood, enters Left. She carries a suitcase.)*
20 NONA: **Think you can take any of my gold, Mr.**
21 **Gardener! Well, you can't! And I'll teach my father**
22 **a lesson, too! I'll run away! And he'll miss me so**
23 **bad he'll never say "no" to me again!** *(She picks up*
24 *the backpack and exits Right.)*
25 LEO: *(Jumping up)* **Sigmund! She stole our gold! Hurry!**
26 SIGMUND: *(Rising)* **Exactly what she was supposed to**
27 **do!**
28 *(The curtain falls.)*
29
30 **Scene Three**
31
32 *A short time later in the Magical Forest. Played before*
33 *the curtain, but this time there is no rock.*
34 *(AT RISE: NONA enters Right carrying suitcase and*
35 *backpack. She looks around nervously.)*

1 NONA: *(Frightened, but resentful)* **This place is sooo**
2 **scary! All these dead trees and horrible rocks! If**
3 **my daddy weren't so mean, I'd never have had to**
4 **run away like this!**
5 *(TROLL enters Right.)*
6 TROLL: **Fee fie fool fold ... I smell a bag of gold!**
7 NONA: *(Unimpressed)* **Oh, it's you.**
8 TROLL: **Give me your gold!**
9 NONA: **Not on your life, buster!**
10 TROLL: **Give me your gold, or I'll turn you into a rock!**
11 NONA: **Do you know who I am?**
12 TROLL: **I only know you have gold. Gold I must take**
13 **for the magician's greedy daughter.**
14 NONA: **I am the magician's greedy daughter! I mean**
15 **daughter. I am *not* greedy!**
16 TROLL: **You are not the magician's greedy daughter!**
17 **She would be in her golden coach with twelve**
18 **servants. She has everything she wants.**
19 NONA: **Lots you know about it! Now, get out of my**
20 **way!**
21 TROLL: **Give me your gold!** *(TROLL grabs for backpack.)*
22 NONA: **Get away from me!** *(She crosses in front of*
23 *TROLL, moving Right.)* **Get away!**
24 TROLL: **I will turn you into a rock!**
25 NONA: **I can run faster than you! I can!** *(TROLL begins*
26 *spinning his hand, and NONA begins spinning*
27 *helplessly to Right.)* **Help! Help!**
28 *(TROLL, laughing, follows her Off Right. LEO and*
29 *SIGMUND enter Left.)*
30 LEO: *(Terrified)* **Sigmund! Hurry! He's going to turn her**
31 **into a rock!**
32 SIGMUND: *(Stopping, thinking)* **Wait!**
33 LEO: **What's wrong?**
34 SIGMUND: **I hope I can remember the spell for**
35 **conjuring up cream puffs!**

1   *(They exit Right as lights dim.)*

2

3   **Scene Four**

4

5   *The Magician's garden, the following morning. Flowers*

6   *now burst from the pots, and the tree is covered with*

7   *leaves and flowers. A "rock" sits Downstage.*

8   *(AT RISE: LEO waters the flowers. SIGMUND sits on*

9   *bench, his feet on the "rock.")*

10 LEO: Someone's coming!

11   *(SIGMUND jumps up, hides behind the tree.*

12   *MILBURN frantically enters Left. He looks all around.)*

13 MILBURN: *(Desperately)* Where can she be?

14 LEO: Who are you looking for, Mr. Magician, sir?

15 MILBURN: Nona? She's gone!

16 LEO: She's right under your nose, sir.

17 MILBURN: I don't see her! Oh, my poor child ... I

18   never should have said "no" to her! Where can she

19   be?

20 LEO: Believe me, Mr. Magician, sir ...

21 MILBURN: *(Near tears)* She's run away ... I never

22   should have given you half of the gold! *(Becoming*

23   *angry)* You're the cause of all this! If you hadn't

24   been so greedy — ! Why, I ought to turn you into

25   a toad!

26 LEO: Please, Mr. Magician, sir! I tell you, your

27   daughter is right in this garden!

28 MILBURN: *(Horrified)* You! You're a magician! You've

29   turned her into something! What? A bug? A blade

30   of grass? A weed? Where is she? Where is Nona?

31 LEO: I'm no magician, sir ... and I have done nothing

32   to your daughter.

33 SIGMUND: *(Appearing from behind the tree)* It was the

34   Troll, Milburn!

35 MILBURN: *(Curiously, surprised)* Sigmund? Is that you?

1   SIGMUND: It is!

2   MILBURN: I thought you'd run away!

3   SIGMUND: I tried to outsmart your Troll ... but I

4   ended up spending several years as a rock ... just

5   like your poor daughter.

6   MILBURN: *(Horrified)* No! You mean —

7   SIGMUND: Nona ran into the forest last night ... we

8   brought her back here because we thought she'd

9   add a nice touch to the garden. *(SIGMUND points*

10   *to "rock.")*

11   MILBURN: *(Heartbroken)* Nona? Nona, is it really you?

12   *(He kneels behind the "rock.")* Oh, my poor daughter,

13   this is all my fault! I never should have given you

14   everything you wanted! I destroyed you! If only

15   you could come back! If only ... *(He begins to cry.)*

16   I can't imagine what life will be like without you

17   here at the castle. My poor little girl! Poor Nona!

18   *(The "rock" moves.)* But wait! What's this? *(NONA*

19   *rises, no longer a "rock.")* Nona! It's you! You're alive!

20   NONA: Daddy? Oh, Daddy, I thought I'd end up a rock

21   forever! It was horrible!

22   SIGMUND: Gets pretty old sitting around in one

23   position all day, doesn't it?

24   NONA: Sigmund? Oh, I'm so glad to see you! And I'm

25   so sorry about sending you away.

26   MILBURN: *(To SIGMUND)* But you said — *(To NONA)*

27   You sent Sigmund away?

28   NONA: He told me I was so greedy and demanding

29   that I was ruining you and everything around me.

30   MILBURN: *(To SIGMUND)* How dare you talk to my

31   daughter that way.

32   NONA: It's OK, Daddy. Sometimes the truth hurts. I

33   had a whole night to think about it. And I've been

34   wrong. People who love us are the most important

35   thing in the world ... not the things we have.

Mystery of the Magical Forest

1   (*GERTRUDE enters Left followed by TROLL who carries*
2   *the treasure chest. GERTRUDE carries her basket.*)
3 GERTRUDE: Stop it, you greedy monster! You've
4   already eaten too many of these things! You'll get
5   a bellyache!
6 TROLL: Cream puff! I want cream puffs!
7 MILBURN: Halt, Troll!
8   (*The TROLL stops.*)
9 GERTRUDE: Thank you, Mr. Magician, sir. I heard
10   you were looking for a cook. I make the best
11   cream puffs in the land.
12 TROLL: Cream puff! I want a cream puff!
13 MILBURN: That's testimony enough for me! You're
14   hired.
15 NONA: And Father! Look at our beautiful garden!
16 MILBURN: Why, in all the excitement, I hadn't noticed.
17   My good Leo, you have done splendid work!
18 LEO: Thank you, Mr. Magician, sir.
19 MILBURN: (*Picking up treasure chest*) Here is your
20   payment.
21 LEO: I will only take what's mine. Return the rest to
22   its owners. (*LEO pulls his bag of coins out of the
23   chest.*)
24 NONA: You are most generous, Mr. Gardener.
25 LEO: (*Bashfully*) Thank you. And please, call me Leo.
26 NONA: Will you be staying with us as our gardener,
27   Leo?
28 LEO: I would like to go to the city and seek my
29   fortune. But may I return to visit?
30 NONA: (*Anxiously*) We would like that, wouldn't we,
31   father?
32 MILBURN: Any time!
33 LEO: Just promise the Troll will stay out of the forest.
34 MILBURN: Fear not! Troll, from now on, you will be
35   the new coachman.

1   TROLL: Really? I don't have to hide in the forest and
2   rob people all day?
3   MILBURN: Never again!
4   TROLL: Thank you, Mr. Magician, sir! You don't know
5   how awful it is having to scare people. Deep down
6   inside, I'm really just a cream puff!
7   *(ALL laugh as the curtain falls.)*

For Better or Worse

Synopsis:
How can a devoted young wife trying to overcome a checkered past save herself and her husband from disgrace? She won't receive any help from her husband's doting sister or from the mysterious stranger who is bent on blackmail.

Characters (2 male, 4 female):
MOLLY CANTRELL, a young wife
ELENA CANTRELL, her sister-in-law
MADAME DELACROIX, a mysterious visitor
JUDGE AVERY CANTRELL, Molly's husband
PRECIOUS PEALE, a society reporter
DETECTIVE JENKINS

Setting:
The parlor of the Cantrell home in a large American city, circa 1900. Fireplace Up Center set with hollow-bottom candlesticks on the mantel. Chairs on either side of the fireplace. Table Down Left set with two chairs. Atop table is a box that locks.

Props:
Newspaper; feather duster; key; box containing papers and news clippings; purse for Madame; elegant, glittering necklace; hollow-bottom candlesticks; tea tray; teacup and saucer; jacket with needle and thread; notepad and pencil; note.

Costumes:
Turn-of-the-century period dress for all. Long dresses for the female characters. Elena should wear an apron. Madame is expensively dressed and can wear a cape and hat. Suit for Avery, overcoat for Jenkins.

Sound Effect:
Knocking on door as indicated in the script.

1	Scene One
2	
3	*The parlor, an afternoon.*
4	*(AT RISE: MOLLY stands Center reading newspaper.*
5	*ELENA enters Right with feather duster.)*
6	ELENA: So much bad news these days.
7	MOLLY: Yes.
8	ELENA: Several more jewel thefts! One just can't keep
9	precious items around without having them stolen,
10	can one? *(ELENA begins dusting.)*
11	MOLLY: Elena, I've asked you to stop cleaning the
12	house.
13	ELENA: I must earn my keep, Mrs. Cantrell.
14	MOLLY: That's ridiculous! Avery and I are happy to
15	have you living here with us.
16	ELENA: But I've always kept Avery's house. Why
17	should his marriage make any difference?
18	MOLLY: I can tend to the work.
19	ELENA: Absolutely not. As wife of a federal judge, you
20	will have increasing social obligations and won't
21	have time for such mundane drudgery as dusting
22	and dishes.
23	MOLLY: I've done my share.
24	ELENA: That's right. You were raised in dire poverty
25	by a woman who never even claimed to be your
26	mother.
27	MOLLY: I know you find that almost impossible to
28	believe —
29	ELENA: *(Too sweetly)* It doesn't matter what I believe,
30	does it? *(A hardness in her voice)* Avery swallowed it
31	all. Hook, line, and sinker!
32	MOLLY: I'm ... I'm sorry you hate me so. If I've ever
33	given you reason ...
34	ELENA: You don't have to! Your being here in this
35	house is reason enough!

1   MOLLY: Your brother and I love each other. It's why
2   we married.
3   ELENA: He married for what he thought was love, I'm
4   sure. But he's always been a bit naive about the
5   world. You? I think it goes without saying that you
6   saw an opportunity to escape prison!
7   MOLLY: That is not true!
8   ELENA: No? *(ELENA moves to box on table. She takes out*
9   *a key and unlocks it. She draws papers from it.)*
10   Shortly before you married, I hired a detective —
11   MOLLY: You did what?
12   ELENA: To look into your background. After all, I
13   knew from the moment I met you —
14   MOLLY: You had no right!
15   ELENA: I have every right to protect my brother!
16   MOLLY: From me?
17   ELENA: From anyone who would in any way harm his
18   reputation!
19   MOLLY: I would have told you everything if you'd only
20   asked.
21   ELENA: I doubt that.
22   MOLLY: I've told Avery everything.
23   ELENA: *(Ominously)* Everything? *(ELENA waves papers*
24   *in front of MOLLY.)* How many times were you
25   arrested, Mrs. Cantrell?
26   MOLLY: I ... I don't remember.
27   ELENA: At least a dozen, according to my source.
28   Petty theft, pickpocketing, loitering, attempted
29   robbery —
30   MOLLY: I was thrown out of my house when I was
31   twelve. That's when my mother — and I use the
32   term loosely — felt we should begin to make our
33   own way in the world. That's how she put it. Make
34   our own way. I did what I could to survive.
35   ELENA: Oh, and then here's an arrest for grand theft.

1   You stole five hundred dollars from an heiress
2   while she was ice skating in the park. She'd left
3   her purse on a bench and you just ... helped
4   yourself. Unfortunately for you, two children saw
5   you and ran to get the police. They locked you up
6   for that one!
7   MOLLY: *(With some dignity)* And those were the best
8   two years of my life!
9   ELENA: You can't be serious!
10   MOLLY: I had a bed! I had two meals a day — even if
11   they were slop, I didn't have to worry about where
12   they were coming from. And at night I was warm
13   most of the time ... something I hadn't had since I
14   was eleven years old.
15   ELENA: So touching. And then there was this business
16   with Mrs. Lowery's jewels. She'd actually given
17   you a job out of the goodness of her heart. She
18   took you in, fresh from jail, cleaned you up, put
19   you to work. And how did you repay her? By
20   stealing her finest pieces of jewelry!
21   MOLLY: I never stole anything from her!
22   ELENA: A ruby ring ... an emerald necklace ...
23   MOLLY: That's a lie!
24   ELENA: ... and an amethyst pendant worth several
25   thousand dollars.
26   MOLLY: I never touched Mrs. Lowery's jewelry!
27   ELENA: Or so you say.
28   MOLLY: I was never convicted.
29   ELENA: Only because you caught my brother's eye.
30   MOLLY: No!
31   ELENA: Don't lie to me! You knew what you were
32   doing! From the moment you saw him, you decided
33   to weave your wicked spell around the poor man
34   and snare him like a helpless rabbit.
35   MOLLY: I never even spoke to your brother until a

1   year after the trial!

2   ELENA: I don't believe it! He was the judge in your

3   case. I don't believe for a moment you didn't

4   figure out how to get into his chambers somehow

5   and give him your sob story.

6   MOLLY: You are so wrong! How could I have done

7   such a thing? And even if I did, it could have

8   resulted in a mistrial and disbarment for your

9   brother and prison for me! The truth is Avery

10   recognized me at a coffee shop where I'd found

11   work. I thanked him for his belief in me ... and he

12   said he was pleased I was working.

13   ELENA: Fool that he was!

14   MOLLY: He began coming in every day ... just to see

15   how I was, I think. And then one day he asked me

16   to dinner.

17   ELENA: *(Disgusted)* Yes, yes, I know the rest of the

18   story.

19   MOLLY: *(Pointing to the papers)* Avery knows all of this.

20   ELENA: Does he?

21   MOLLY: And even if he didn't, we are husband and

22   wife now.

23   ELENA: Yes ... a nice touch running off and getting

24   married without a word to me!

25   MOLLY: We wanted our privacy. We didn't want the

26   newspapers knowing.

27   ELENA: I can see why!

28   MOLLY: All that is in the past. It's forgotten.

29   ELENA: It will never be forgotten, my dear. *(ELENA*

30   *locks the papers in the box.)*

31   MOLLY: What do you intend to do with that

32   information?

33   ELENA: I'm sure the readers of the *Post* and *Tribune*

34   would love a few juicy details about you.

35   MOLLY: You would never turn that over to the press.

1   You would hurt Avery's reputation worse than
2   mine.
3 ELENA: I would if you ever do anything to harm
4   Avery.
5 MOLLY: What?
6 ELENA: *(Patting the top of the box)* This is my insurance
7   policy. The moment you make one false step, I will
8   see to it that your entire sordid past is revealed.
9 MOLLY: I am not that person any longer! I despise
10   myself for having stolen and pickpocketed to make
11   a living. If I could pay back every penny I took,
12   I'd gladly do so.
13 ELENA: How easy to say with my brother's money.
14 MOLLY: You don't believe me, do you?
15 ELENA: Once a thief, always a thief!
16   *(A knock is heard Off Right.)*
17 MOLLY: I'll go.
18 ELENA: Please. Don't trouble yourself. *(ELENA exits*
19   *Right. A moment later she returns with MADAME*
20   *DELACROIX.)*
21 MADAME: Actually, it was Mrs. Cantrell I wanted to
22   see.
23 ELENA: Mrs. Cantrell, Madame Delacroix.
24 MOLLY: How do you do?
25 ELENA: I'll make some tea.
26 MADAME: That won't be necessary.
27 ELENA: No trouble at all. *(ELENA exits Left.)*
28 MOLLY: Would you like to sit down? *(MADAME does so.)*
29   How may I help you?
30 MADAME: My situation is a very delicate one.
31 MOLLY: Go on.
32 MADAME: I have a dear friend who has been unjustly
33   accused of a crime.
34 MOLLY: Unjustly?
35 MADAME: Yes. He has been accused of a theft, but he

1   was nowhere near the place where the crime
2   occurred at the time it was supposed to have
3   happened. They say he stole some jewels ... but it's
4   ridiculous!
5 MOLLY: I don't see how I can help you.
6 MADAME: My dear ... your husband is the trial judge.
7 MOLLY: There's absolutely nothing —
8 MADAME: You don't seem to recognize me, do you?
9 MOLLY: Perhaps ... vaguely ...
10 MADAME: I knew you when you were thirteen,
11   fourteen years old. You stayed in my attic.
12 MOLLY: No! Letty Bonds?
13 MADAME: Please! I am so much more respectable
14   these days. I no longer deal with youthful
15   pickpockets. I married a Frenchman, Monsieur
16   Delacroix, who almost had a title.
17 MOLLY: Don't you realize that what you're asking me
18   is wrong?
19 MADAME: Isn't it also wrong to send a man to prison
20   for something he didn't do?
21 MOLLY: You can't be sure he didn't do it.
22 MADAME: Of course I can! He never stole anything,
23   the poor dear. I did! *(From her purse, MADAME*
24   *pulls a beautiful, glittering necklace.)*
25 MOLLY: The Jacard Necklace! *(MOLLY grabs the*
26   *newspaper she was reading.)* Stolen from Mrs.
27   Benton Jacard's home six months ago ... never
28   found ...
29 MADAME: I'd been trying so hard to just pass by such
30   baubles ... but this one called my name, and when
31   I saw it lying on her dressing table during a party
32   at her mansion ... I just knew I had to have it. I
33   slipped it into my purse, never realizing my dear
34   friend would be accused.
35 MOLLY: I'm afraid this is a matter for the police.

```
1    MADAME: Why get them involved? They're all so
2       stupid. You merely need to have a little talk with
3       your husband.
4    MOLLY: I can't do that!
5    MADAME: Express an interest in the case. Say that
6       you don't think the accused is guilty.
7    MOLLY: Never!
8    MADAME: And gradually you'll bring the good judge
9       around to your way of thinking. There really isn't
10      enough evidence to convict him.
11   MOLLY: My husband would never listen to me.
12   MADAME: (Coyly) I think he would do anything you
13      wanted!
14   MOLLY: No! Don't say that! And I think it's time you
15      left.
16   MADAME: I will make it worth your while. (MADAME
17      lays the necklace on the table.)
18   MOLLY: Take that thing with you! You said you
19      couldn't live without it.
20   MADAME: (Shrugging, pleased) I'll always know it's
21      mine. But if it will save my dear friend ... I gladly
22      give it to you.
23   MOLLY: (Grabbing the necklace) I don't want this!
24   MADAME: I will stop by tomorrow to see how you are
25      getting along with your husband.
26   MOLLY: I won't do a thing to influence him! It's
27      bribery, and I plan to call the police immediately
28      and tell them the entire story.
29   MADAME: Then I shall be forced to give every detail
30      of our business relationship. Then and now! My
31      mere presence here in your house along with your
32      background will be enough to ruin your husband
33      forever. He'll be disbarred and left to the vultures
34      of the press. Good day, my dear! Until tomorrow.
35      (MADAME extends her hand cordially, but MOLLY
```

turns away. *MADAME exits Right. MOLLY hesitates, then hides the necklace under one of the hollow candlesticks on the mantel. ELENA sees this as she enters Left with tea tray.)*

ELENA: **Molly!** *(MOLLY turns quickly, frightened.)* **Your guest didn't wait for tea! Well, I will say you look like you could use a cup. You're deathly pale!** *(ELENA sets tray on table, smirking, as the curtain falls.)*

Scene Two

The same, that evening.

(AT RISE: AVERY stands holding tea cup. ELENA sits sewing a button on a coat.)

AVERY: **She seemed fine this morning.**

ELENA: **She's quite a delicate creature. She says even the fumes from soap make her dizzy, so I take care of the kitchen. But I don't mind. Any other sewing that needs to be done, Avery?**

AVERY: **No.**

ELENA: **Then I'd best get to dusting! It's amazing how much dust falls on everything.** *(ELENA begins dusting.)* **Poor Molly just coughs and coughs when she tries to dust.**

AVERY: **She told me that she almost died when she was eighteen. She'd caught a respiratory infection during the winter because she was living in a small shack —** *(Suddenly angry)* **It doesn't make sense how we can be so cruel to the weakest people! It's so easy to look down on them and say it's their fault. They should have worked harder, they should have gone to school, they should scrub themselves up! It's not simple at all. The only simple thing is to see why some must resort**

1   to a life of crime.

2 ELENA: I'm sure you're right. And so tragic when they

3   do fall into that abyss and they can never really

4   climb their way out of it. No matter how hard they

5   try.

6 AVERY: What do you mean?

7 ELENA: Take your dear Molly, for example.

8 AVERY: What about her?

9 ELENA: She has worked so hard at overcoming all the

10   horrors of her upbringing and all those years and

11   years as a …

12 AVERY: Thief? Is that the word you're looking for?

13 ELENA: Oh, Avery, Molly means everything to me.

14   Heaven knows I'm not a name-caller, but we can't

15   deny that she was convicted once —

16 AVERY: I know, Elena. Perhaps we should leave all

17   this where it belongs. In the past.

18 ELENA: That's just it, Avery. Yesterday the past came

19   calling.

20 AVERY: What are you talking about?

21 ELENA: I don't know if I should say anything —

22 AVERY: Then don't. *(AVERY sits and picks up newspaper*

23   *to read.)*

24 ELENA: A woman came to see your wife.

25 AVERY: What woman?

26 ELENA: She said her name was Madame Delacroix.

27 AVERY: An old friend?

28 ELENA: I'm not sure. I left the room to make tea and,

29   of course, I didn't hear what they talked about.

30 AVERY: I hope, then, they had a pleasant visit.

31 ELENA: I don't believe the visit was merely social.

32 AVERY: *(Folding paper, standing nervously)* What are you

33   trying to tell me, Elena?

34 ELENA: As I brought the tea into the room, Madame

35   Delacroix was just leaving and … and …

1   AVERY: Go on.
2   ELENA: Oh, Avery, I don't know how to tell you this,
3   but in her hand Molly held the Jacard necklace.
4   AVERY: You must be mistaken.
5   ELENA: I didn't believe it at first, but the light caught
6   the large center diamond and practically blinded
7   me!
8   AVERY: Why would Molly have something so valuable?
9   ELENA: And dangerous!
10 AVERY: *(Shaking his head)* Your eyes were just playing
11   a trick on you, Elena, that's all. You mistook what
12   you saw for the Jacard necklace. It was probably
13   just some new bauble Molly bought for herself.
14 ELENA: Your wife doesn't spend money on herself,
15   Avery.
16 AVERY: Perhaps it's a gift for someone else.
17 ELENA: She ... she hid it under that candlestick.
18 AVERY: Elena, stop this!
19 ELENA: If you don't believe me, look!
20 AVERY: This is absurd!
21 ELENA: If anyone finds that here, we'll all be arrested!
22 AVERY: Elena, there is no necklace under that
23   candlestick!
24 ELENA: Even if *we* are not blamed, you'll be ruined.
25 AVERY: Stop it!
26 ELENA: Do you want me to show you?
27 AVERY: No!
28 ELENA: Please, Avery, I don't want her to destroy you!
29 AVERY: Molly would never —
30 ELENA: *(Firmly)* Lift that candlestick!
31   *(AVERY moves to candlestick. He looks at ELENA, then*
32   *reaches out to it just as MOLLY enters Left.)*
33 MOLLY: Avery!
34 AVERY: *(Drawing his hand away)* Molly, my dear! What
35   a delicious dinner tonight.

1   MOLLY: Thank you.

2   ELENA: The next time you try to cook a chicken, my

3   dear, you'll need to let me show you how to sear

4   the skin first.

5   *(A knock is heard Off Right. ELENA rises and looks*

6   *out the window.)*

7   MOLLY: Are you expecting anyone, Avery?

8   AVERY: No ... it's already been a long day.

9   ELENA: Oh, dear! I'm afraid I totally forgot!

10   AVERY: Forgot what?

11   ELENA: A newspaper writer, a Mrs. Peale, stopped by

12   today and asked if it would be all right if she

13   asked you a few questions this evening. I tried to

14   fend her off, but she was quite insistent.

15   AVERY: Elena, you know I can't discuss a trial with

16   the press.

17   ELENA: She's a society editor.

18   AVERY: Society?

19   ELENA: Probably wants to speak with Mrs. Cantrell as

20   well. Perhaps a few questions on your wedding

21   and how you newlyweds are doing.

22   *(Another insistent knock is heard.)*

23   MOLLY: *(With a glance at ELENA)* We'd best not keep

24   her waiting, then!

25   ELENA: *(With a smirk)* Yes, Ma'am. *(ELENA exits Right.)*

26   AVERY: Odd time for an interview, I must say.

27   MOLLY: She'll probably be looking for something very

28   juicy ... a scandal, perhaps.

29   PRECIOUS: *(From Off Right)* All set, then? I've done

30   everything —

31   *(ELENA shushes PRECIOUS as both enter Right.*

32   *PRECIOUS carries a notepad.)*

33   ELENA: Mrs. Peale, this is my brother, Judge Avery

34   Cantrell.

35   PRECIOUS: I am so pleased to meet you! You're every

1   bit as handsome as they said you'd be!
2   AVERY: This is my wife, Mrs. Peale.
3   PRECIOUS: Oh, call me Precious! That's my given
4   name. It really is! My editor loves it! My column's
5   titled "Precious Tidbits." That's what I hope to get
6   here tonight. A bit of your life together, how you
7   met, and so on.
8   MOLLY: I'm afraid we're a terribly dull couple, Mrs.
9   Peale.
10 ELENA: Oh, come, come. You've had quite an exciting
11   life.
12 AVERY: My sister reads too many romances. Our real
13   lives, as my wife said, are very dull. You see how
14   we spend our evenings ... reading the paper,
15   playing backgammon. *(A knock is heard Off Right.)*
16   And so many visitors is highly unusual.
17 ELENA: I can't imagine who that can be.
18 MOLLY: *(Looking out the window)* Madame Delacroix.
19 AVERY: Who?
20 ELENA: Your friend who stopped by earlier?
21 PRECIOUS: Madame Delacroix? Now where have I
22   heard that name before?
23 ELENA: *(Exiting Right.)* We can only imagine.
24 MOLLY: I think it would be best if you'd take Mrs.
25   Peale into the study where she can ask her
26   questions, my dear. I have something to discuss
27   with Madame Delacroix.
28 AVERY: *(Glancing at the candlestick)* Molly, I need to
29   know something —
30 MOLLY: Later, my dear. *(MOLLY gently moves AVERY*
31   *Left.)*
32 AVERY: *(Taking the hint)* This way, Mrs. Peale. *(AVERY*
33   *and PRECIOUS exit Left as ELENA leads MADAME*
34   *On Right. MADAME carries a small purse.)*
35 MADAME: Ah, Mrs. Cantrell! What a pleasure it is to

1   see you again.

2   MOLLY: Elena, would you please leave us for a few

3   moments?

4   ELENA: Where have you sent Avery and his guest?

5   MOLLY: They're in the study. I'm sure you can add a

6   great deal to whatever Avery is telling that

7   reporter.

8   ELENA: An excellent idea. *(ELENA exits Left.)*

9   MADAME: A reporter, here, at this hour?

10   MOLLY: They have no respect for privacy anymore.

11   MADAME: I received your note and came immediately.

12   I assume you have mentioned my friend's case to

13   your husband?

14   MOLLY: I did not send you a note.

15   *(From her purse, MADAME pulls out a paper.)*

16   MADAME: You didn't send this?

17   MOLLY: No. And I have not mentioned the case at all

18   to my husband.

19   MADAME: You aren't serious.

20   MOLLY: I am.

21   MADAME: I expressly told you that —

22   MOLLY: I will not help you!

23   MADAME: You think I won't follow through on my

24   word? You have a reporter in there right now who

25   would love to find out every bit of dirt on you!

26   MOLLY: You don't frighten me.

27   MADAME: I don't imagine I do. What would frighten

28   someone who spent years on the street stealing

29   from hardworking folks? And then years in prison

30   where they teach you even more tricks about how

31   to destroy society!

32   MOLLY: Aren't you being rather hypocritical, Madame

33   Delacroix? And I have never been concerned with

34   destroying society. *(MOLLY, Upstage now from*

35   *MADAME, slips the necklace back into MADAME's*

1   *purse, which sits on the table next to MADAME's chair.)*
2   MADAME: I see ... then just destroying one man is
3   enough.
4   MOLLY: I would never do anything to hurt Avery.
5   MADAME: Then convince him that my friend is
6   innocent.
7   MOLLY: I don't have to!
8   MADAME: What are you talking about?
9   MOLLY: You've already admitted to stealing the
10   necklace.
11   MADAME: I never said any such thing!
12   MOLLY: You stood here yesterday and said you took it
13   while at a party at the Jacard home.
14   MADAME: I'm afraid you're lying.
15   MOLLY: I think not.
16   MADAME: Then I must call your bluff, my dear. I am
17   going to the papers immediately.
18   MOLLY: Why not let the paper come to you? *(MOLLY*
19   *moves Left.)* Mrs. Peale! Mrs. Peale! Come in here,
20   please, will you?
21   MADAME: *(Nervously)* What are you doing?
22   MOLLY: Mrs. Peale will be glad to get the whole story
23   from you.
24   *(ELENA, PRECIOUS, and AVERY enter Left.)*
25   PRECIOUS: What's wrong, Mrs. Cantrell?
26   MOLLY: Madame Delacroix has something to tell you.
27   ELENA: You can't be serious, Molly!
28   AVERY: What's this all about?
29   ELENA: I've already told you, Avery.
30   MOLLY: What has your sister told you?
31   AVERY: Nothing I'd believe.
32   ELENA: *(Hurt, angered)* I see, Avery. I see very clearly!
33   *(ELENA exits Left.)*
34   PRECIOUS: Do you have a story for the paper,
35   Madame?

1 MADAME: This woman is a fraud. *(She glares at*
2 *MOLLY.)*
3 AVERY: How dare you! Leave this house at once!
4 PRECIOUS: What, exactly, do you mean, "a fraud"?
5 MADAME: She began her life as a pickpocket and
6 petty thief. She eventually graduated to grand
7 theft.
8 PRECIOUS: A dull couple, indeed!
9 AVERY: I don't know who you are, Madame, but stop
10 these slanderous allegations!
11 MADAME: Every word can be proven.
12 PRECIOUS: Is this true, Mrs. Cantrell?
13 AVERY: Molly, don't say a word!
14 MOLLY: It's all right, Avery. Yes. Every word can be
15 proven.
16 PRECIOUS: *(Scribbling furiously on notepad)* Oh,
17 gracious me!
18 AVERY: Please, Mrs. Peale, everything that happened
19 is in the past ... long forgotten. Whatever my wife
20 did to survive the terrible years after her mother
21 threw her out of the house has been paid for time
22 and time again!
23 MADAME: That would all be fine if she had stopped
24 her life of crime.
25 AVERY: What do you mean, "if"?
26 PRECIOUS: You're saying that she is still a thief?
27 AVERY: Get out of here at once!
28 *(ELENA enters Right, followed by DETECTIVE*
29 *JENKINS.)*
30 JENKINS: I'm afraid nobody's going anywhere.
31 ELENA: The necklace is here, Detective Jenkins.
32 AVERY: Elena! I can't believe you'd do such a thing!
33 ELENA: You're being used, Avery. Can't you see that?
34 She's using you, and if she's not stopped now, you
35 will be ruined.

1   JENKINS: Look, I'm not interested in family squabbles —
2   PRECIOUS: But I am!
3   JENKINS: I got a tip that the Jacard necklace is in
4   this house. And I want it handed over!
5   MADAME: You're absolutely right, Detective. It is here!
6   *(Indicating MOLLY)* This woman stole it from the
7   Jacard residence.
8   JENKINS: *(To MOLLY)* Is that true, Ma'am?
9   *(MOLLY says nothing.)*
10 ELENA: It's under the candlestick, Detective.
11 AVERY: *(Moving to mantel, blocking the way)* No!
12 ELENA: I saw her put it there!
13 JENKINS: *(To MOLLY)* Would you mind lifting the
14   candlestick, Ma'am? Now I don't have a search
15   warrant, so I can't officially look. But you can
16   save me the trouble of getting a warrant by just
17   turning over the necklace.
18   *(MOLLY doesn't move.)*
19 ELENA: Just like I thought! Guilty! *(ELENA moves to*
20   *candlestick, but AVERY blocks her way.)*
21 AVERY: I can't believe you're doing this!
22 ELENA: Move, Avery! Let me show you once and for
23   all what kind of woman you married!
24   *(AVERY pushes ELENA gently aside and lifts the*
25   *candlestick. There is nothing under it.)*
26 AVERY: I know what kind of woman I married. *(He*
27   *moves to MOLLY.)* She's not a thief.
28 ELENA: *(Furiously)* Then she moved it!
29 PRECIOUS: Where?
30 ELENA: I don't know!
31 MOLLY: I do not have the Jacard necklace.
32 JENKINS: Then who does?
33 MOLLY: The thief.
34 JENKINS: I don't know what this is all about, but
35   somebody got me here under false pretenses!

1   ELENA: No! She's got it somewhere! I know it! Or else
2   you already sold it. Is that it? You sold it so you
3   can run off leaving my poor brother in ruins?
4   MOLLY: *(Weakly)* Oh, Avery ... oh ... *(MOLLY faints.)*
5   AVERY: Molly! Molly!
6   JENKINS: She's just fainted. Here, now ... you got
7   smelling salts in your purse? *(JENKINS grabs*
8   *MADAME's purse.)*
9   MADAME: Really, Detective! Of course I've got
10   smelling salts, but you needn't be so abrupt!
11   *(JENKINS pulls Jacard necklace from MADAME's*
12   *purse.)*
13 JENKINS: Well, I'll be!
14 PRECIOUS: Those don't look like smelling salts!
15 AVERY: The Jacard necklace!
16 ELENA: That can't be!
17 MADAME: I ... I've never seen that thing before in my
18   life!
19 ELENA: She had it yesterday!
20 JENKINS: And now we've got you red-handed!
21 AVERY: Molly, are you all right?
22 MOLLY: Yes ... yes ... what's happened?
23 ELENA: You know what happened.
24 MOLLY: I don't. What's she talking about, Avery?
25 AVERY: I don't think she even knows!
26 JENKINS: I'm taking you in for questioning, Madame!
27 MADAME: *(To MOLLY)* You are so clever, my dear!
28   Someone taught you very well.
29 JENKINS : Come along, now, and leave these people in
30   peace! *(JENKINS exits Right with MADAME.)*
31 PRECIOUS: Mrs. Cantrell ... did you plan all this?
32 MOLLY: Oh, Mrs. Peale, I couldn't do that. I'm just a
33   very dull housewife who loves my husband more
34   than anything.
35 PRECIOUS: I'll return tomorrow for a follow-up! Right

1   now, I'm going after that detective and thief! I

2   want her story in detail! Thank you, Elena ... I'm

3   so glad you set this up for tonight!

4 AVERY: I'll see you out, Mrs. Peale. And when I

5   return, I want to have a chat, Elena. A long chat.

6   *(AVERY exits Right with PRECIOUS.)*

7 ELENA: How did you do it?

8 MOLLY: Do you think pickpockets can only take

9   things *out* of a purse?

10 ELENA: You think you're so clever.

11 MOLLY: No, but one thing I've learned, Elena, is how

12   to survive. Avery and I will weather every storm

13   because we truly love each other. You'll never

14   understand that, and I feel very sorry for you.

15   *(AVERY enters Right as ELENA moves Left.)*

16 AVERY: Elena! Where are you going?

17 ELENA: To pack. *(ELENA exits Left.)*

18 MOLLY: I'm sorry, Avery ... I didn't mean to give you

19   a scare.

20 AVERY: Molly ... I never doubted you for a minute!

21   *(They embrace as the curtain falls.)*

Mommy's a Zombie!

Synopsis:
A farce is a comedy built on mistaken identities and misunderstandings. Generally a farce contains a lot of physical action, quick lines, and seemingly hopeless confusion until everything works out magically in the end. Here, see how mistaken identities threaten to undo a surprise for a hardworking mother.

Characters (3 male, 8 female):
TESS OSBORNE, 30s, mom, teacher, play director
FRANKIE OSBORNE, 14, Tess's oldest son
ROBIN OSBORNE, 10, Tess's youngest daughter
PAM, a young actor
TOBY, another young actor
HEATHER, another young actor
WENDY, another young actor
JOSH, another young actor
MRS. BROADFOOT, 50s, a neighbor
PEGGY POST, 20s, works at the State Department of Education
MINDY WIGGINS, 20s, a reporter

Setting:
The basement of the Osborne house. Wing entrance Down Left leads to the upstairs; wing entrance Down Right leads to laundry room and backyard. Boxes stacked up here and there, a few old toys, an old card table set up Down Right, a few chairs, and sheets stretched across ropes Upstage drying.

Props:
Basket of wash; two cellphones; sandwich; small pad of paper and pencil; camera.

Costumes:
Everyday dress for all characters. Mrs. Broadfoot dresses more old-fashioned than the others, wearing a flower-print dress and a shawl. In second scene, Tess wears a Zombie Queen costume: a long black or white dress, fright wig, oversized red or black fingernails, and so on.

Sound Effects:
Small dog barking, cellphone ring.

1	**Scene One**
2	
3	*(AT RISE: TESS stands Center holding a basket of*
4	*wash. MRS. BROADFOOT stands to her right. ROBIN*
5	*is hiding behind one of the sheets hanging Upstage. We*
6	*hear a small dog barking.)*
7	MRS. BROADFOOT: *(Angry)* It's too late, Mrs. Osborne!
8	I have had enough of your precious little Polly!
9	TESS: But she's such a sweet little dog, Mrs. Broadfoot.
10	I don't understand it!
11	MRS. BROADFOOT: She has bitten me three times!
12	And you know the old football saying — three
13	strikes, you're out!
14	TESS: I'm sorry ... but I don't see any bites on you.
15	MRS. BROADFOOT: She bit my foot! My foot is in my
16	shoe! Of course you can't see where she bit me.
17	But I am in pain, Mrs. Osborne! Pain! And for all
18	I know, that mutt has rabies!
19	TESS: Oh, no, that mutt — I mean Polly — got her
20	shots just last week. The animal control people
21	don't even understand how she bit you.
22	MRS. BROADFOOT: Whenever she runs loose she
23	attacks me! I live in constant fear next door! I
24	want you to get rid of that monster today!
25	*(ROBIN jumps out from behind one of the sheets.)*
26	ROBIN: No! We can't get rid of Polly, Mom! We won't
27	let you!
28	TESS: I'm sure Mrs. Broadfoot didn't really mean that.
29	MRS. BROADFOOT: I certainly did! And I have
30	contacted a reporter from the *Plopsville Post* who is
31	coming to do a story about that vicious animal.
32	TESS: A reporter? Mrs. Broadfoot, that's totally
33	uncalled for!
34	MRS. BROADFOOT: I intend to do anything to get that
35	beast out of this neighborhood! If for no other

1   reason than to enjoy some peace and quiet! *(MRS.*
2   *BROADFOOT moves Right.)*
3   TESS: Oh, don't go out that way. Polly's in the
4   backyard. *(FRANKIE enters Right.)* Polly is tied up,
5   isn't she, Frankie?
6   FRANKIE: Yeah. She doesn't like it, but she won't get
7   away.
8   MRS. BROADFOOT: I'll believe that when I see it!
9   Remember, Mrs. Osborne, get rid of that dog, or
10   I'll press charges! *(MRS. BROADFOOT moves Left,*
11   *but is looking back at TESS. MRS. BROADFOOT*
12   *walks into a sheet.)* Oh, goodness! *(ROBIN and*
13   *FRANKIE laugh.)* How do I get out of here?
14   TESS: The door's right through there. *(TESS points the*
15   *way.)*
16   MRS. BROADFOOT: *(To FRANKIE and ROBIN)* Laugh
17   all you like, but if I could I'd be rid of the lot of
18   you! *(MRS. BROADFOOT exits Left.)*
19   FRANKIE: Can I let Polly go now, Mom?
20   TESS: I don't know, Frankie. If she goes into Mrs.
21   Broadfoot's yard again —
22   ROBIN: She only goes over there because the old bat —
23   TESS: Robin! That isn't nice!
24   ROBIN: Well, it's not nice of her putting cookies out so
25   she can tease Polly and then get her in trouble.
26   TESS: Is that what she does?
27   FRANKIE: At least once a day!
28   TESS: Well, once we get through tomorrow, we can
29   take care of Mrs. Broadfoot! I just need to keep
30   my focus on the play — and this laundry. I sure
31   wish the dryer still worked!
32   ROBIN: We ought to just buy another one.
33   TESS: A couple of more pressing expenses, kiddo, like
34   the car getting fixed. Uncle Bill said we can have
35   his old one as soon as his new one gets shipped.

1   ROBIN: *(Hinting)* Hey, Mom, maybe you'll get rich all
2   of a sudden.
3   TESS: *(With a smile)* I have bought a lottery ticket
4   recently. Right now I've got to check the prop list
5   to make sure we've got everything we need for the
6   play.
7   ROBIN: It's gonna be great, Mom. Your shows always
8   are.
9   FRANKIE: And everybody likes zombie plays. Patty's
10   gonna be a great Zombie Queen.
11   ROBIN: Yeah, she looks like a ghost. Today after
12   school she looked positively green!
13   TESS: Well, let's keep our fingers crossed that all our
14   zombies and ghouls know their lines! *(Phone rings.*
15   *TESS pulls out and opens her cellphone.)* Hello? ...
16   Yes, this is Mrs. Osborne. ... Oh, hi, Mrs. Peters.
17   Are you helping Patty with her lines? ... The
18   hospital? Oh, no! ... Oh, no! ... Oh, I understand
19   completely, Mrs. Peters. You tell Patty we're all
20   rooting for her! ... Thank you. Goodbye. *(Puts away*
21   *phone.)*
22   FRANKIE: I wonder if this is how the people felt when
23   the Titanic hit the iceberg.
24   ROBIN: What's wrong, Mom?
25   TESS: Patty didn't just look green today when you saw
26   her, Robin. She *was* green. She's got appendicitis,
27   and they're operating on her right now.
28   ROBIN: I'm glad it's not tomorrow! She's got a play to
29   do.
30   FRANKIE: Dingledorf! She won't be all better
31   tomorrow! She'll still be in the hospital.
32   ROBIN: Don't call me Dingledorf!
33   TESS: Kids! Listen ... I've got to think of something
34   fast, and your arguing won't help. Robin ... do you
35   think you could learn her part?

1   ROBIN: Sure!
2   FRANKIE: Mom, Patty has two hundred and fifteen
3   lines!
4   ROBIN: *(Sheepishly)* Two hundred? I ... I could learn
5   half of 'em.
6   FRANKIE: *(Sarcastically)* And everybody could go
7   home at intermission.
8   TESS: *(Disappointedly)* Well, if there's no one to play the
9   part ... we might have to cancel.
10 FRANKIE: You can't do that, Mom! After all our
11   practices! *(With sudden enthusiasm)* Hey! Why don't
12   *you* play the Zombie Queen?
13 TESS: *(With a laugh)* Me?
14 ROBIN: You sure the school board wouldn't mind a
15   teacher turning into a zombie?
16 TESS: I *do* know the lines ... and that way ... I
17   wouldn't be letting you kids down.
18 ROBIN: *(Sarcastically)* Are you sure you can remember
19   two hundred and fifteen lines? Old people are
20   sooo forgetful!
21 TESS: Who said I'm that old?! But we'll need to have
22   an emergency rehearsal. Tonight.
23 FRANKIE: Uh oh! The auditorium's being used for the
24   spelling bee until tomorrow afternoon.
25 TESS: All right. We could use my classroom.
26 FRANKIE: No way! They waxed the floors this
27   weekend, remember?
28 TESS: Frankie, you're not being very helpful!
29 FRANKIE: How about here? We've got enough room.
30 TESS: *(Looking around the room)* I guess we could ... but
31   it's a mess ...
32 ROBIN: They're supposed to be zombies. What do they
33   care about messes?
34 TESS: I'll go call the cast and get them over here.
35   Good thing I have Patty's costume here. I just

1   hope it fits! *(Now reciting lines)* **Oh, so you are the**
2   **new guests at the Zombie Hotel! I am blooody glad**
3   **to meet you!** *(TESS laughs wickedly as she exits Left.)*
4   FRANKIE: Wow, what a trooper!
5   ROBIN: Mom's a teacher, not a cop!
6   FRANKIE: A trooper is somebody who's like a hero!
7   ROBIN: Oh! Well, this'll sure help her win the Tip Top
8   Teacher Award.
9   FRANKIE: Shhh! That's a surprise! Nobody's supposed
10   to know but us and the principal. You almost
11   spilled the beans when you asked about getting
12   rich quick!
13   ROBIN: Well, she's going to win, isn't she? And then
14   she'll get five hundred dollars, right?
15   FRANKIE: *(Crossing his fingers)* She's a finalist. There's
16   just one last interview.
17   ROBIN: An interview?
18   FRANKIE: Yeah ... the principal told me today somebody
19   would be stopping by to ask Mom a few questions.
20   ROBIN: But then she'll figure it out.
21   FRANKIE: No, the interviewer kind of acts like she's
22   taking a survey or something. You know ... so the
23   answers are completely honest.
24   ROBIN: Honest?
25   FRANKIE: Honest, Dingledorf!
26   *(ROBIN screams at FRANKIE and chases him Off*
27   *Right as the curtain falls.)*
28
29   **Scene Two**
30
31   *The same, an hour later.*
32   *(AT RISE: PAM, TOBY, HEATHER, FRANKIE, and*
33   *TESS are at Center rehearsing. ROBIN sits on boxes*
34   *Left. TESS wears Zombie Queen costume; others are in*
35   *street clothes. They use Dracula accents when they are*

1   *rehearsing their parts.)*
2   TESS: And then I come in and say ... *(As the Zombie*
3   *Queen)* The new guests are here, Dr. Danger!
4   TOBY: *(As Dr. Danger)* Excellent! It's always good to
5   have some new blood around the old place!
6   PAM: I know! My last meal was vegetarian, and it just
7   didn't stick to my ribs!
8   HEATHER: Can we go up now for a bite?
9   FRANKIE: Let's at least give them a chance to get
10   comfortable in their red cells!
11   TESS: OK ... and then Wendy is supposed to say —
12   *(WENDY and JOSH enter Left. JOSH is eating a*
13   *sandwich.)*
14   WENDY: *(As a zombie)* Excuse me, but we're looking for
15   our room.
16   JOSH: *(With his mouth full)* 'Cause we sure are pooped!
17   TESS: That line would be a lot clearer if you weren't
18   eating a sandwich, Josh.
19   JOSH: Dinner. We were just sitting down when you
20   called.
21   TESS: Oh, I'm sorry. But we've got to have this
22   rehearsal because Patty's in the hospital.
23   PAM: She has appendicitis.
24   TOBY: Is that bad?
25   HEATHER: They have to cut you open!
26   WENDY: Kinda like our play.
27   JOSH: Who's playing her part, then?
28   FRANKIE: Mom's going to.
29   WENDY: Really? That's cool!
30   TESS: I hope I do OK.
31   TOBY: You gonna bite me in the neck?
32   TESS: I'll fake it, Toby.
33   TOBY: Whew! Patty kept saying she was really going
34   to rip me to shreds!
35   PEGGY: *(Calling from Off Left)* Yoo hoo! Anybody home!

1   **FRANKIE:** Shhh!
2   **TESS:** Oh, no! That must be the reporter from the *Post!*
3   **PEGGY:** *(Calling from Off Left)* **Are you downstairs?**
4   **FRANKIE:** *(Thinking quickly)* **Robin! Keep her busy!**
5   **ROBIN:** Me?
6   **FRANKIE:** Yeah! You can talk the paint off a wall!
7   **TESS:** We'll go outside and rehearse. Tell her the dog
8   is out back, and she doesn't like anybody coming
9   in her yard. *(TESS herds ALL Off Right. ROBIN*
10   *follows.)*
11   **ROBIN:** *(Exiting Right)* **Guys! You can't leave me here**
12   with the press!
13   *(When ROBIN is gone, PEGGY enters Left. She is*
14   *carrying a small pad and pencil. She's talking on her*
15   *cellphone.)*
16   **PEGGY:** Jen, I don't think anybody's home at the *(She*
17   *checks her pad)* **Osborne's. This could delay the**
18   selection of a winner a day or so, OK? I'll have to
19   come back. *(ROBIN enters Right.)* **Maybe not!**
20   *(PEGGY snaps her phone shut.)* **Why, hello, there.**
21   Are you home alone?
22   **ROBIN:** *(Nervously)* **I ... ah ... Mom's not here.**
23   **PEGGY:** Oh, dear! It's important that I talk to her. My
24   name's Mrs. Post.
25   **ROBIN:** *Post,* **huh? Well, I can tell you everything you**
26   need to know.
27   **PEGGY:** Really?
28   **ROBIN:** Yup! 'Cause she's mine as much as anybody's.
29   **PEGGY:** Really? Well, then perhaps you can answer a
30   few questions. *(PEGGY sits at the card table.)*
31   **ROBIN:** *(With growing confidence)* **Shoot.**
32   **PEGGY:** How about education? Where did she go to
33   school?
34   **ROBIN:** Canine Academy.
35   **PEGGY:** Canine Academy? What ... what did she

1   learn there?

2   ROBIN: Everything! Like how to sit, roll over, heel.

3   PEGGY: Excuse me, but are we talking about the same

4   person?

5   ROBIN: Gosh, you're a whole lot nicer than Mrs.

6   Broadfoot! She'd never call her a person.

7   PEGGY: Who's Mrs. Broadfoot?

8   ROBIN: The lady next door.

9   PEGGY: Why wouldn't she call her a person?

10   ROBIN: She says that she bit her.

11   PEGGY: Bit her? Good heavens!

12   ROBIN: If she did, and I seriously doubt it, it's because

13   Mrs. Broadfoot puts out cookies, and then once

14   she's in Mrs. B.'s yard, Mrs. B. snatches the

15   cookies away just to tease her.

16   PEGGY: Can't she buy her own cookies?

17   ROBIN: Oh, we've got lots of treats for her. But you

18   know how these special little ladies are.

19   PEGGY: I do?

20   ROBIN: Sure! They want whatever they can't have.

21   PEGGY: I understand now that she's quite an actress.

22   ROBIN: Oh, she's great at howling and whining.

23   PEGGY: What about directing? What's her style?

24   ROBIN: She just leads, and we all follow.

25   PEGGY: That's good. And is she well liked?

26   ROBIN: Everybody just loves her! Especially the kids.

27   PEGGY: She's a good listener?

28   ROBIN: She sure is. You can tell her anything, and she

29   won't say a word.

30   PEGGY: I imagine that all the kids trust her, then.

31   ROBIN: Oh, everybody trusts her except for Mrs.

32   Broadfoot.

33   PEGGY: Does Mrs. Broadfoot have any children in

34   school?

35   ROBIN: The only thing Mrs. Broadfoot has is a parrot

1	named Squeaky. And it's a real talker. I went over
2	there once to deliver Christmas cookies, and
3	Squeaky said "Get lost! Get lost!" just like that.
4	*(FRANKIE, PAM, TOBY, HEATHER, WENDY, and*
5	*JOSH enter Right and sneak behind the sheets.)*
6	PEGGY: Not very friendly.
7	ROBIN: I'll say. Hey, how come you're so nice?
8	PEGGY: Why shouldn't I be nice?
9	ROBIN: Frankie said reporters aren't nice and ask too
10	many questions!
11	PEGGY: A reporter? But, my dear, I'm —
12	*(The kids move like zombies from behind the sheets,*
13	*arms outstretched, staring straight ahead, heavy*
14	*accents.)*
15	FRANKIE: Help us!
16	PAM: Hungry!
17	TOBY: We are hungry!
18	*(PEGGY, half frightened, half amused, rises, leaving*
19	*her tablet on the table.)*
20	PEGGY: Well, now ... what do we have here?
21	ROBIN: *(With mock terror)* Oh, gosh! We've got to get out
22	of here!
23	PEGGY: Children ... you're all very cute, but ... I ... I
24	hope you're only fooling! *(PEGGY moves Left.)*
25	ROBIN: They're zombies! They'll kill both of us!
26	FRANKIE: We just woke up!
27	PAM: Tired and hungry!
28	ROBIN: Gosh, that's a pretty bad combination!
29	PEGGY: Now stay away from me! Get back! Get back!
30	*(PEGGY races Off Left shouting "Help! Help!" The*
31	*kids follow her, laughing.)*
32	HEATHER: *(Still a zombie)* Come back!
33	WENDY: We will get you!
34	JOSH: There's no escaping the Zombie Queen!
35	*(ROBIN follows them all Off Left. TESS enters Right*

1   *and moves to Center.)*
2   **TESS: Did you get rid of that reporter, kids? Kids?**
3   *(TESS moves behind one of the sheets as PEGGY*
4   *nervously enters Left. She moves to the table and picks*
5   *up her tablet. At the same time, TESS steps from*
6   *behind sheet and backs to Center. PEGGY, sensing*
7   *someone is coming Left, backs to Center. In a moment,*
8   *TESS and PEGGY back into each other, turn, and*
9   *scream. PEGGY faints into a chair just as ROBIN,*
10   *FRANKIE, PAM, TOBY, HEATHER, WENDY, and*
11   *JOSH enter Left.)*
12 **ROBIN: Boy! She won't come here again looking for a**
13   **story!**
14 **FRANKIE: Are you all right, Mom? You are Mom,**
15   **aren't you?**
16 **TESS: Oh, Frankie! This poor woman's fainted. Robin,**
17   **run and get a glass of water.**
18 **PAM: Hey, this is great!**
19 **TOBY: If you're that good at being the Zombie Queen,**
20   **you'll scare the whole audience.**
21 **TESS: Ma'am ... are you all right? Ma'am?**
22 **HEATHER: Aren't you supposed to put her head**
23   **between her legs?**
24 **WENDY: That's what they taught us in health class.**
25 **TESS: That might work.** *(TESS pushes PEGGY'S head*
26   *between her legs. PEGGY moans.)* **Take a few deep**
27   **breaths.**
28 **PEGGY:** *(Gasping)* **I can't ... I can't ...**
29 **TESS: Yes, you can!**
30 **PEGGY: I can't breathe like this!**
31 **TESS:** *(Releasing PEGGY)* **Oh! Sorry!**
32   *(PEGGY slowly sits up.)*
33 **JOSH: Gosh, you sure got scared!**
34 **ROBIN: Maybe you better get in your car and drive**
35   **back to your newspaper!**

1   PEGGY: My what?
2   TESS: Look, we know you were here to do a story on
3   our dog Polly, and the kids were just trying to
4   help.
5   FRANKIE: Polly never bit anybody!
6   ROBIN: She's really very sweet and gentle.
7   PEGGY: And she went to Canine Academy.
8   ROBIN: Right.
9   PEGGY: *(To ROBIN)* So you were telling me all about
10   Polly, weren't you?
11   ROBIN: Sure! Who'd you think I was talking about?
12   *(MRS. BROADFOOT and MINDY enter Left.)*
13   MRS. BROADFOOT: That screaming can only mean
14   one thing! The dog has struck again, Miss Wiggins!
15   MINDY: I'd better get a look at this creature!
16   MRS. BROADFOOT: At your own peril!
17   TESS: Mrs. Broadfoot? Is there something we can do
18   for you?
19   MRS. BROADFOOT: The screams alerted us! That
20   beast has attacked again, hasn't it?
21   PEGGY: Actually I'm the beast who screamed.
22   TESS: And I helped.
23   MRS. BROADFOOT: Oh, you poor thing. Miss Wiggins
24   ... here's where you start your story! A poor,
25   innocent stranger wandered into a house of
26   horrors ...
27   ROBIN: She's going to write a story?
28   MINDY: Mindy Wiggins from the *Plopsville Post*.
29   FRANKIE: *(Nervously)* You're the reporter?
30   ROBIN: *(Horrified)* Then who are you?
31   PEGGY: Peggy Post from the Tip Top Teacher Award.
32   FRANKIE and ROBIN: Uh oh!
33   TESS: Kids, what's going on?
34   FRANKIE: *(To ROBIN)* Should we tell her?
35   PEGGY: It probably would be a very good idea.

1 FRANKIE: We nominated you for the Tip Top Teacher
2   Award, Mom.
3 TESS: You what?
4 ROBIN: We wanted it to be a surprise.
5 FRANKIE: We didn't have enough money to get you a
6   new dryer.
7 ROBIN: So we thought if you win ...
8 PAM: I think it's a great idea!
9 TOBY: You taught me how to tell a noun from a verb ...
10 HEATHER: And you direct all the plays and
11   everything.
12 WENDY: You're even willing to play the Zombie Queen!
13 JOSH: And I sure wouldn't be caught dead in that
14   outfit.
15 MINDY: So that's why you're dressed up like that!
16 FRANKIE: Patty Peters was supposed to play the part
17   tomorrow night, but she's in the hospital.
18 ROBIN: Appendicitis.
19 MINDY: Hey, this story's a whole lot better than "Dog
20   Bites Man"!
21 MRS. BROADFOOT: Dog bites woman! Me! And I want
22   the entire neighborhood alerted to the menace!
23   They're just trying to divert attention from the real
24   problem here! *(MRS. BROADFOOT moves Right.)* It's
25   right out back! Why, you can see that hideous
26   creature now!
27   *(Dog starts barking.)*
28 FRANKIE: Uh oh! She saw the cookie monster!
29 MRS. BROADFOOT: *(Terrified)* Is that door safe? Can
30   it break through?
31 ROBIN: It did once! Chewed right through the wood!
32 MRS. BROADFOOT: Oh, dear! Get me out of here!
33   *(MRS. BROADFOOT races Off Left as MINDY moves*
34   *Right. Barking stops.)*
35 MINDY: *(Looking out a window Stage Right)* **That's** the

1   vicious monster?

2   PAM: Cute little thing, isn't it?

3   MINDY: It's a Chihuahua!

4   PEGGY: Isn't there some saying about it's not the size
5   of the bite but the sound of the bark that matters?

6   TOBY: *(Notices that TESS looks troubled.)* Gosh, Zombie
7   Queen, what's wrong?

8   TESS: Oh, kids ... you went to all this trouble for me,
9   and I'm so ashamed! I've ruined everything!

10 FRANKIE: It's not your fault, Mom.

11 ROBIN: We should have gotten her picture I.D. right
12   from the start. *(ROBIN indicates PEGGY.)*

13 PEGGY: Well, I should have offered it. It's as much my
14   fault as anyone's.

15 TESS: And here you ended up fainting and everything!

16 PEGGY: Oh, I wasn't really scared ... much.

17 TESS: All I can say is we're so sorry.

18 PEGGY: Nonsense! Just a little misunderstanding. I
19   have had four other interviews today, and they
20   were all exactly the same. I haven't drank so much
21   tea in my life! And you know something? Yours is
22   the only interview which really showed me why
23   you're a Tip Top Teacher!

24 FRANKIE: Way to go, Mom!

25 TESS: But I didn't do anything.

26 PEGGY: Oh, no? Looking at this cast of yours, I think
27   you've done plenty. Your play is going to be a
28   success. Now, I'd better be off and write up my
29   recommendation and leave you to your rehearsal!

30 ROBIN: I guess you wouldn't like any tea, huh?

31 PEGGY: Let's wait 'til the awards ceremony ... *(To
32   ROBIN)* and thank you very much for the
33   interview.

34 ROBIN: No problem! No problem at all!

35 TESS: Goodbye, Ms. Post. Thanks so much for being

1   so understanding!

2   *(PEGGY exits Left.)*

3   **FRANKIE:** *(To MINDY)* **So whatdaya think? You aren't**

4   **gonna do a story on Polly, are you?**

5   **MINDY: I think I'd rather do a story on a Tip Top**

6   **Teacher and her tip top cast. Let's get you all**

7   **together for a photo!** *(The KIDS and TESS group*

8   *themselves quickly, but all look very stern.)* **That's it!**

9   **You all look great, but smile!**

10   **PAM: Zombies don't smile!**

11   **MINDY: I think we can make an exception!**

12   *(ALL smile as MINDY snaps a picture and the curtain*

13   *falls.)*

The Mother Goose Mystery

Synopsis:
When a famous children's book publisher ends up drinking poisoned cocoa, which of the nursery rhyme characters is the killer? It's anybody's guess until a clever trick by Theophilis Thistle flushes out the culprit.

Characters (4 male, 5 female):
MYRNA GOOSE, a publisher
JACK HORNER, Myrna's partner
BETSY MUFFET, Myrna's executive assistant
JENNY WREN, Myrna's housekeeper
BOBBY SHAFTO, Myrna's nephew
MARY LAMB, a writer
TOM PIPER, a mail room employee
DAME TROT, a neighbor
THEOPHILIS THISTLE, a detective

Setting:
The study of Myrna Goose's mansion. A desk Center, fireplace Left, and a pair of chairs with a small table between them Right. A curtained window behind the desk. Above the fireplace hangs an illustrated picture of Mother Goose flying with the words "Mother Goose Children's Books" boldly proclaimed. Wing entrance Left leads to main entrance. Wing entrance Right leads to other areas of the house. A mug of cocoa sits on desk.

Props:
Briefcase; coat; silver piece with polishing cloth; mug of cocoa on desk; contracts on desk; telephone with answering machine on desk; stuffed cat; piece of paper; envelopes containing paychecks; box on fireplace mantel; small leash; two suitcases; videotape; handcuffs; pink slip of paper.

Costumes:
Modern dress for all. Long robe and hood for Tom. A mask can be added to further disguise him.

Sound Effects:
Clock striking eight o'clock (used twice); door slamming (used twice).

Note: Voices on answering machine can either be recorded or the lines can be spoken by an actor Offstage.

1   **Scene One**

2

3   *The study, just before eight o'clock at night.*

4   *(AT RISE: MYRNA enters Left carrying briefcase and*

5   *coat.)*

6   **MYRNA: Jenny! Jenny Wren! Neat as a pin, but late**

7   **again!** *(MYRNA tosses coat and briefcase on chair at*

8   *Left.)* **Where *is* that useless girl?**

9   *(JENNY enters Right polishing silver.)*

10   **JENNY: Good evening, Ms. Goose.**

11   **MYRNA: What's so good about it?**

12   **JENNY: Hard day at the office?**

13   **MYRNA: Impossible! Our latest writer, who my**

14   **editorial staff assured me has some talent —**

15   **JENNY: You mean Mary Lamb?**

16   **MYRNA: Soon to be a household name — but not if she**

17   **doesn't get her book finished on time!** *(Mimicking*

18   *her staff)* **It'll be a bestseller! The children of the**

19   **world are clamoring for her latest creation!** *(As*

20   *herself)* **Ha! They'll have to clamor to another**

21   **publisher!**

22   **JENNY: But she signed a contract.**

23   **MYRNA: She missed her deadline ... so sorry, Mary**

24   **Lamb, pack your fleece and go! I noticed**

25   **footprints all over the walk. Did the men replacing**

26   **the oven get the job done?**

27   **JENNY: They didn't show up, Ma'am.**

28   **MYRNA: What? They promised!**

29   **JENNY: Your nephew stopped by.**

30   **MYRNA: Bobby Shafto, back from the sea? What'd he**

31   **want? Another handout?**

32   **JENNY: He didn't say, Ma'am.** *(MYRNA moves to chair*

33   *behind the desk.)* **And your partner Jack Horner**

34   **stopped by with those papers to sign.**

35   **MYRNA:** *(Picking up contracts from desk)* **If he thinks**

1   Mother Goose Books is going to merge with Father
2   Time, Inc., he's crazy! *(She notices something on the*
3   *chair.)* Ahhh! What's this?
4 JENNY: Oh, dear! It looks just like ...
5 MYRNA: *(Disgusted)* Cat hair!
6 JENNY: Dame Trot stopped by to fetch one of her cats!
7 MYRNA: You let a cat in this house?
8 JENNY: No, Ma'am, I didn't!
9 MYRNA: Then how is it my chair is covered with cat
10   hair? You *had* to have let it in, you foolish girl!
11 JENNY: No, Ma'am ... the doors were closed like you
12   want, and all the windows were shut. It must have
13   found some other way in!
14 MYRNA: The fact that Dame Trot keeps ten cats
15   wouldn't bother me if she kept them at home! But
16   when they start clawing and pawing their way
17   over here, it's time to call the cops! *(MYRNA picks*
18   *up her phone.)* Oh, did Betsy Muffet stop by with
19   the paychecks?
20 JENNY: No, Ma'am, but —
21 MYRNA: What? I've got to sign them tonight, or none
22   of you will get paid tomorrow! What *is* it about
23   this staff of mine?
24 JENNY: Ms. Goose, she had Tom Piper deliver them
25   for her.
26 MYRNA: Who's Tom Piper?
27 JENNY: The piper's son. He works in the mail room.
28   The checks are right on your desk there.
29 MYRNA: You could have said that in the first place,
30   Jenny. Why can't somebody make my life easier?
31 JENNY: Will there be anything else, Ma'am?
32 MYRNA: No ... go finish whatever you're wasting your
33   time on. *(JENNY exits Left. MYRNA picks up cocoa*
34   *and smiles. She takes a sip, likes the taste, and has a*
35   *bit more. She takes contracts and tosses them into the*

1   *fireplace. She drinks more cocoa, then turns on her*
2   *answering machine.)*
3 **VOICE ON MACHINE: Sorry you're not in, Myrna. It's**
4   **Margery Daw seeing if you want to go shopping**
5   **Saturday. Call me and let me know!**
6   *(MYRNA presses button.)*
7 **VOICE ON MACHINE: Hello! I'm calling from**
8   **Amalgamated Life Insurance. Is your coverage up-**
9   **to-date? If not —**
10   *(MYRNA pushes button.)*
11 **VOICE ON MACHINE: Hickory, dickory, dock ... the**
12   **mouse ran up the clock. The clock struck eight, for**
13   **you it's too late ... hickory, dickory ... death!**
14 **MYRNA:** *(Angry)* **Of all the stupid ... Jenny! Jenny**
15   **Wren!**
16   *(The clock strikes eight as JENNY enters Left.)*
17 **JENNY: Yes, Ma'am?**
18 **MYRNA: Change our phone number! Some nut's**
19   **leaving crazy messages!**
20 **JENNY: Again, Ma'am? Perhaps the police could —**
21 **MYRNA: Change it tomorrow! And, oh, this cocoa has**
22   **a funny aftertaste. What did you put in it?**
23 **JENNY: I never made any cocoa, Ms. Goose.**
24   *(A door slams Offstage Right.)*
25 **MYRNA: Then what —** *(A look of horror, a grimace, and*
26   *MYRNA falls to the floor as JENNY screams. Blackout*
27   *or quick curtain.)*
28
29   **Scene Two**
30
31 *The same, the following afternoon.*
32   *(AT RISE: THEOPHILIS THISTLE sits on edge of*
33   *desk. BOBBY SHAFTO stands by fireplace. BETSY*
34   *MUFFET sits in chair, weeping. JACK HORNER*
35   *stands in a corner. DAME TROT sits in other chair*

1   *petting a stuffed cat. JENNY stands uncomfortably in*
2   *corner opposite JACK. TOM PIPER stands near her.)*
3 BETSY: I can't believe Myrna Goose is ... gone.
4 BOBBY: Poor Aunt Myrna! The old bat.
5 BETSY: How can you say that?
6 BOBBY: She was an old bat. A nasty, conniving old
7   battle-ax who had it coming to her.
8 JACK: Careful, Bobby. Detective Thistle is taking all
9   this down!
10 BOBBY: You think he isn't going to find out about her?
11 DAME: I always say, "Speak nothing but good of the
12   dead."
13 JENNY: Especially when ....
14 THISTLE: Go on, Ms. Wren. "Especially when" what?
15 JENNY: Nothing.
16 THISTLE: I take it Ms. Goose and Dame Trot here
17   didn't get along too well?
18 DAME: *(Defensively)* We got along as fine as any
19   neighbors do in the modern world.
20 JACK: Meaning you were at each other's throats
21   constantly.
22 DAME: If she'd only kept an open mind about some
23   things.
24 JENNY: She hated those cats of yours! She told you,
25   but they wouldn't stop coming over here.
26 DAME: Once, maybe twice, one of them strayed over
27   here ... and took her paws in her life doing so, I'll
28   tell you!
29 JENNY: *(Incredulously)* Once or twice!
30 BETSY: They were always over here, Detective Thistle.
31 TOM: I almost stepped on one yesterday when I came.
32 JENNY: The same one that got in here and made a
33   mess on her chair. She was calling the police, you
34   know, when ... when .... *(JENNY begins to cry.)*
35 DAME: That's ridiculous!

1   THISTLE: Not really. She'd already made a number of
2   complaints, and, if I've read the records right, one
3   more complaint and the animal protection agency
4   was going to pay you a visit, Dame Trot.
5   DAME: Let them! My cats are perfectly happy. *(To cat)*
6   Aren't you, precious? *(To THISTLE)* You know,
7   Detective Thistle, every one of these people had a
8   better motive to kill Myrna Goose than I did.
9   THISTLE: You think so?
10 JENNY: Not me. I was devoted to her.
11 BOBBY: The way she treated you? I can't imagine she
12   kept you in clover, the stingy old bat.
13 JENNY: My salary was adequate.
14 THISTLE: That's not true, Ms. Wren. She paid you fifty
15   dollars a week.
16 JENNY: Plus room and board.
17 JACK: You call that closet under the stairs a room?
18 JENNY: I ... I don't really ... need more.
19 THISTLE: She was blackmailing you, wasn't she?
20 JENNY: Blackmail? What are you talking about?
21 THISTLE: When you first applied for work here she
22   had Ms. Wren investigated, didn't she, Ms. Muffet?
23 BETSY: She had all her employees investigated.
24 THISTLE: What did she find?
25 BETSY: You lied on your application, Jenny.
26 JENNY: No!
27 BETSY: You never did graduate from Tittlemouse
28   College. You'd cheated on a final exam and were
29   expelled.
30 THISTLE: So she gave you the option of working here
31   for nothing or being found out.
32 BOBBY: *(Laughing)* Jenny Wren! Everybody cheats on
33   tests! What would it matter to you?
34 JENNY: I was the first person in my family who ever
35   graduated from college. Fortunately none of my

1   family could make it to graduation, so I just told
2   them I graduated and then got a job on the
3   editorial staff of Mother Goose Books.
4 BETSY: You poor thing.
5 JENNY: I've worked for her for two years. Why would
6   I kill her now?
7 THISTLE: Oh, I intend to find out.
8 JACK: Really, Detective, this was probably some
9   maniac off the street or something. You're acting
10   like we're all suspects or something.
11 THISTLE: A maniac who leaves hot cocoa, Mr.
12   Horner? *(Pushes button on answering machine.)*
13 VOICE ON MACHINE: Hickory, dickory, dock ... the
14   mouse ran up the clock. The clock struck eight, for
15   you it's too late ... hickory, dickory ... death!
16 BETSY: How awful!
17 JACK: That was on her machine?
18 THISTLE: *(Nodding)* Doesn't sound like the work of a
19   random killer, does it?
20   *(JACK shakes his head.)*
21 JENNY: Last night she told me to change the phone
22   number again. Now I see why.
23 TOM: She got a lot of prank calls?
24 THISTLE: Not just calls, but letters as well.
25 DAME: Threatening letters?
26 JACK: She *was* very hard to work for.
27 BETSY: Demanding on her authors —
28   *(MARY LAMB rushes in Left.)*
29 MARY: Oh, dear! I'm late! I'm so sorry.
30 THISTLE: Quite all right, Ms. Lamb, isn't it?
31 MARY: Yes.
32 JACK: Our latest author.
33 JENNY: Not according to Ms. Goose.
34 THISTLE: Oh?
35 JENNY: She said Ms. Lamb missed her deadline, and

1   her contract wasn't any good anymore.

2 JACK: Not again!

3 MARY: Oh, dear ... I was just finishing the last

4   chapter. Surely she wouldn't have ...

5 JACK: *(Sweetly)* I wouldn't let that happen, Mary.

6 BETSY: But she would have! She cancelled contracts

7   of several big authors who didn't get work done

8   on time.

9 THISTLE: Of course, Ms. Lamb, you won't have to

10   worry about that now.

11 JACK: Exactly!

12 THISTLE: I understand Mother Goose Books now

13   belongs solely to you, Mr. Horner.

14 BOBBY: Stuck in his thumb, pulled out a plum, and

15   said "What a rich boy am I!"

16 BETSY: Really, Mr. Shafto!

17 BOBBY: It's true, isn't it?

18 JACK: It's standard procedure when one partner dies,

19   the remaining partner inherits the other's share.

20 THISTLE: So now you can go ahead with the Father

21   Time, Inc. merger.

22 JACK: If the board OKs it.

23 THISTLE: A merger Ms. Goose was definitely against.

24   We found the contracts in the fireplace ready to be

25   burned.

26 JACK: Maybe she didn't put them there.

27 JENNY: She did! She was right there when I came into

28   the room ... ready to light them.

29 JACK: *(Defensively)* All right! So now we can move

30   Mother Goose Books into the twenty-first century.

31   Is that so wrong? Maybe you ought to look

32   elsewhere for a motive ... like gambling debts.

33   *(JACK glares at BOBBY.)*

34 BOBBY: Oh, please! That's old news. Everyone knows

35   I hit on auntie once in a while to keep my silver

1   buckles shiny. But I held my own.

2   THISTLE: This time you needed over thirty thousand

3   dollars ... not exactly chicken feed.

4   BOBBY: Where'd you hear that?

5   THISTLE: Word on the street.

6   BOBBY: Yeah? Well, why would I kill the goose who

7   laid the golden egg?

8   THISTLE: Because the goose was worth more to you

9   dead than alive.

10   BOBBY: *(Nervously)* What ... what do you mean?

11   THISTLE: Ms. Goose left you this estate, her cars, and

12   almost everything else aside from the company.

13   BOBBY: *(Smiling)* Why, dear, dear Aunt Myrna!

14   BETSY: How do you know that?

15   THISTLE: I read the will. It was right in this desk.

16   BETSY: But I think she just changed it.

17   THISTLE: Really?

18   BETSY: She'd contacted her lawyer, and I witnessed

19   the signing of certain papers. I'm almost sure one

20   said "Last Will and Testament."

21   THISTLE: Where is it?

22   BETSY: I don't know. She signed it at her office.

23   THISTLE: Do you know the provisions?

24   BETSY: She didn't tell me.

25   THISTLE: *(Cautiously)* Maybe she'll tell us on the

26   videotape.

27   JACK: *(Nervously)* What videotape?

28   THISTLE: The police received this message from Ms.

29   Goose last week. *(From his pocket he pulls a piece of*

30   *paper. Reads.)* "My life is in danger. Repeated

31   telephone messages, e-mails, and regularly mailed

32   notes indicate someone wants me dead. If I die

33   under mysterious circumstances, the videotape I

34   have made will reveal my suspicions."

35   BOBBY: *(With a laugh)* I don't believe it for a second!

1   JENNY: A videotape?

2   TOM: Where is it?

3   BETSY: I never saw any videotape.

4   JACK: Why wouldn't she just tell you who she thought

5   was sending the messages?

6   THISTLE: Simple!

7   MARY: She didn't want to accuse the wrong person.

8   DAME: Ms. Goose? Worried about someone else's

9   reputation?

10   BOBBY: That's a laugh!

11   THISTLE: More worried about her own reputation. If

12   word had gotten out about the threats, she

13   wouldn't have been in a very strong bargaining

14   position regarding the merger.

15   *(Sound of door slamming is heard Offstage Right.)*

16   BETSY: What was that?

17   JENNY: We heard that last night just before ... before ...

18   *(THISTLE runs Off Right.)*

19   JACK: Hold on! You might need help! *(JACK follows Off*

20   *Right.)*

21   BOBBY: You know something? I think I'll have this

22   room redone in chartreuse. Careful everyone, don't

23   scratch my furniture! *(BOBBY exits Left.)*

24   BETSY: He did it! I know it!

25   TOM: I'm going to trail him and find out just where

26   he's headed.

27   DAME: That could be dangerous.

28   TOM: I can take care of myself.

29   BETSY: Tom!

30   TOM: I said I can take care of myself! *(TOM races Off*

31   *Right as THISTLE enters Left.)*

32   DAME: Find anything, Detective?

33   THISTLE: Must have been the wind.

34   JENNY: It wasn't the wind last night. It was the killer!

35   BETSY: Still in the house?

1   THISTLE: Had to be. The cocoa was still hot.

2   DAME: *(Rising)* But I'm afraid your trail is a bit cold.

3   If you need me, I'll be feeding my cats currant

4   buns and cherry tarts. *(DAME exits Right.)*

5   BETSY: And I must get the paychecks signed by Mr.

6   Horner. *(BETSY takes checks from desk.)* Is he out

7   back?

8   THISTLE: I believe he noticed some footprints in the

9   garden.

10   JENNY: *(To THISTLE)* Shouldn't you be looking at

11   them?

12   THISTLE: *(Shrugging)* This killer has left better clues

13   than footprints, Ms. Wren.

14   JENNY: *(Nervously)* What ... what do you mean?

15   BETSY: You know who the killer is?

16   THISTLE: It's just a matter of time.

17   MARY: Are we free to leave?

18   THISTLE: Oh, of course. This wasn't anything official.

19   Just a casual ... get-together. *(BETSY exits with*

20   *paychecks.)* You may go about your business, Ms.

21   Wren.

22   JENNY: You need me again, you know where to find

23   me. *(JENNY exits Left.)*

24   MARY: Detective, there's something I need to tell you ...

25   THISTLE: *(Holding his fingers to his lips)* Sorry, Ms.

26   Lamb, but I've had an emergency call and must

27   get back to town. Meet me here tonight at eight.

28   You can tell me then.

29   *(THISTLE leads MARY Off Right. JENNY enters*

30   *Left, begins looking about the room. She hears someone*

31   *coming and hides behind curtains. JACK enters, looks*

32   *about, crosses to Right, exits. BETSY enters Left, moves*

33   *to desk, looks through drawers, hears someone coming,*

34   *and hides under or behind desk. MARY enters Right,*

35   *checks over fireplace, looks behind picture. She exits*

1   *Left. DAME enters Right. She checks over room, moves*
2   *Right, but bumps into BOBBY as he enters Right.)*
3   BOBBY: Did our little party break up?
4   DAME: Why ... yes ... yes ... it did. I forgot Hannah
5   Bantry's toy. *(DAME holds up cat toy she's taken from*
6   *her pocket.)*
7   BOBBY: She wouldn't want to be without her toy,
8   would she? *(DAME hurries Off Right.)* So, Auntie
9   Goose? Wither didst thou put that video? Upstairs?
10   Downstairs? Or in thy lady's chamber?
11   *(BOBBY laughs, exiting Left. BETSY races Off Right*
12   *from behind desk. JENNY slips from behind curtains*
13   *and exits Right as the curtain falls.)*
14
15   **Scene Three**
16
17   *The same, eight o'clock that night.*
18   *(AT RISE: The room is empty and dimly lit. The clock*
19   *chimes eight. A moment later, DAME enters Left*
20   *carrying a small leash.)*
21   DAME: Mistress Mary? Mistress Mary? Why must you
22   be so contrary?
23   *(JENNY enters Right.)*
24   JENNY: Dame Trot! What are you doing in here?
25   DAME: Mistress Mary, my gray tabby, has run off.
26   JENNY: How did you get in?
27   DAME: The front door is unlocked.
28   JENNY: Unlocked! It can't be! I locked it myself just a
29   short while ago. *(JENNY moves Left as BOBBY*
30   *enters Left.)*
31   BOBBY: Hello, Jenny, old girl!
32   JENNY: I'm no "old girl" to you. What are you doing
33   here?
34   BOBBY: Moving in. It is my house, after all. What have
35   we here? A party?

1 DAME: I was just looking for Mistress Mary, my tabby.
2 BOBBY: Look away! I've nothing to hide. And you, my
3   fine lady in waiting, go fetch my suitcases from
4   the car.
5 JENNY: I'll do no such thing.
6 BOBBY: Then I'll just have to let that cat out of the
7   bag. *(Angrily, JENNY exits Left.)* So, your Mistress
8   Mary isn't in here ... maybe she's downstairs. The
9   mice are bigger there.
10 DAME: Yes, I suppose she might be.
11 BOBBY: I'll lead the way. *(BOBBY moves Right. DAME*
12   *hesitates.)* It's quite all right. I wouldn't hurt a fly.
13 DAME: I ... I think I'll go home. If you see her, just
14   give me a call. She's a big, gray tabby.
15   *(DAME rushes Off Left. BOBBY laughs, exits Right. A*
16   *moment later JENNY enters Left with JACK and*
17   *MARY. JENNY has a suitcase in each hand.)*
18 JENNY: *(Setting suitcases down)* I don't know where she
19   would have put a computer disc. Anywhere, I
20   imagine.
21 MARY: This is her study, isn't it?
22 JENNY: She called it that.
23 JACK: But there's no computer.
24 JENNY: She always used her laptop. She kept it in her
25   briefcase. It was right here last night. *(JENNY*
26   *picks up briefcase, now sitting next to desk.)* Yes, here
27   it is.
28 JACK: Let's have a look, then.
29 MARY: You think it's all right?
30 JACK: The police would have sealed off the room if
31   they didn't want us looking in here.
32 JENNY: They said they were done with the place.
33 JACK: Thank you for your help, Ms. Wren.
34 MARY: Do you need help with those bags?
35 JENNY: No, they're Mr. Shafto's. He's moving in, and

1   he travels light.
2   JACK: Until now. Hard to believe this is all his.
3   JENNY: It's hard not to believe. He and his aunt were
4   cut from the same cloth, if you ask me. *(JENNY*
5   *exits Right.)*
6   JACK: *(Opening briefcase)* Let's have a look.
7   MARY: Mr. Horner, there's no laptop in the briefcase.
8   JACK: And not a computer disc in sight.
9   MARY: Maybe it's upstairs in her bedroom. Lots of
10   people work in their beds.
11 JACK: Somehow I can't picture Mother Goose voiding
12   contracts in the luxury of her bedroom!
13 MARY: I'll go up and have a look.
14 JACK: Better let me. Shafto might get a bit upset
15   seeing someone sneaking around. *(JACK exits*
16   *Right.)*
17 MARY: Detective? Detective Thistle? It's after eight.
18   Detective Thistle!
19   *(BOBBY enters Right.)*
20 BOBBY: What are you calling him for?
21 MARY: Why ... I ... I thought he might be here ... and ...
22 BOBBY: And?
23 MARY: I wanted to ask him ... how the investigation
24   was going.
25 BOBBY: Really? Is that all you wanted?
26 MARY: No. We — Mr. Horner and I — need the
27   computer disc with my book manuscript on it.
28 BOBBY: That so?
29 MARY: Your aunt made some corrections, and I need
30   them. I can't finish the manuscript without them.
31 BOBBY: I don't believe a word you're saying.
32 MARY: It's true!
33 BOBBY: This is private property, you know. *My*
34   private property.
35 MARY: Your maid let us in.

1 BOBBY: She shouldn't have done that. But since you're
2   here ... how about you stick around? You're kind
3   of cute.
4 MARY: Oh, I've heard about you, Bobby Shafto!
5 BOBBY: And it's all true.
6 MARY: You go through money like it's nothing.
7 BOBBY: I hear your book's going to make money hand
8   over fist, so we might make a good pair.
9 MARY: Sorry, but I'm really a very dull person.
10   Boring, in fact. Now, if you'll excuse me. *(MARY*
11   *moves Left, but BOBBY steps in her way.)*
12 BOBBY: But you never got to see Detective Thistle.
13 MARY: It's all right. I'll talk to him some other time.
14 BOBBY: About what? What do you know? You see
15   something ... or just imagine you saw something?
16 MARY: No! I didn't see anything! Now let me out of
17   here.
18 BOBBY: C'mon, Mary! You can tell me what you know.
19   After all, she was my aunt.
20 MARY: Get away from me!
21 BOBBY: You're not afraid of me, are you? I wouldn't
22   hurt a fly!
23   *(THISTLE pushes curtain aside and moves to BOBBY.)*
24 THISTLE: You've got that exactly right, Mr. Shafto. I
25   wouldn't let you hurt a fly!
26 BOBBY: Hey, just trying to break the ice, Detective.
27 MARY: *(To THISTLE)* I'm glad to see you!
28 THISTLE: Don't worry. I was here the whole time. And
29   I think I'd like to take Mr. Shafto in for more
30   questioning.
31 BOBBY: You aren't taking me any place!
32 THISTLE: You can either come along voluntarily, or
33   I'll arrest you on suspicion of murder!
34 BOBBY: I didn't — oh, all right ... all right!
35 THISTLE: And on the way to the car, Ms. Lamb, you

1   can tell me what you saw.
2   **MARY:** Oh, I didn't see anything. It's what I heard!
3   *(THISTLE pushes BOBBY Off Left with MARY*
4   *following. A moment later, BETSY enters Right. She*
5   *begins to search the room and, in a box on the mantel,*
6   *finds a videotape. A black-hooded FIGURE enters Left,*
7   *moves quickly behind her and grabs the videotape. She*
8   *struggles for a moment.)*
9   **BETSY:** Give me that! Let go! *(FIGURE pushes BETSY*
10   *down. She screams. FIGURE runs Off Right. THISTLE,*
11   *BOBBY, and MARY enter Left.)*
12   **THISTLE:** Stay with her, Bobby! *(THISTLE runs Off*
13   *Right.)*
14   **BOBBY:** Hey! Since when am I a cop?
15   **MARY:** *(Helping BETSY)* Are you all right?
16   **BETSY:** I think so.
17   **BOBBY:** You just decide to join the party, too?
18   *(JENNY and JACK enter Right.)*
19   **JACK:** What's going on?
20   **BETSY:** Someone attacked me!
21   **MARY:** Did you see who?
22   **BETSY:** No, but I think it was that cat woman!
23   **BOBBY:** Old Dame Trot? Why would she attack you?
24   **BETSY:** Someone ... someone called my office. The
25   voice was very garbled, but it told me where the
26   videotape was.
27   **JENNY:** Ms. Goose's videotape?
28   **BETSY:** The voice said it was hidden in a box on the
29   mantel. I thought if I could find it and get it to
30   Detective Thistle, the case would be solved.
31   *(THISTLE enters Right holding a handcuffed FIGURE.*
32   *THISTLE also holds the videotape.)*
33   **THISTLE:** Oh, it's solved, all right.
34   *(ALL look one to another.)*
35   **BETSY:** That's ... great.

1 JACK: So who is this killer? *(JACK pulls back hood*
2 *revealing TOM.)*
3 BOBBY: *(Laughing)* Tom, Tom, the piper's son ... stole
4 a pig and away did run!
5 MARY: But why?
6 THISTLE: Any reason for killing Ms. Goose, Mr.
7 Piper?
8 *(TOM says nothing.)*
9 JENNY: You left her the cocoa? How could you have
10 known she liked cocoa? You only work in the mail
11 room.
12 THISTLE: It's also a pretty good trick since you didn't
13 have any traces of cocoa in your car.
14 JACK: What are you talking about?
15 THISTLE: During our meeting this morning, our
16 forensics team went through all your cars. We
17 figured whoever brought the cocoa had spilled a
18 bit here and there. And we were right.
19 MARY: But ... but ... anyone could have cocoa in his
20 car.
21 THISTLE: True, but not just anyone would also have
22 been overheard yesterday by you, Ms. Lamb,
23 saying "You try anything like that, and you'll find
24 yourself pushing up daisies."
25 MARY: But I'm sure the voice was —
26 JENNY: Why, Tom? Why?
27 THISTLE: Oh, Mr. Piper didn't have cocoa in his car.
28 And he never threatened anyone.
29 BETSY: But he stole the tape!
30 TOM: I did it for you!
31 BETSY: *(Feigning innocence)* What? That's ... that's
32 ridiculous, Tom.
33 THISTLE: Is it? Love has made men do far more
34 foolish things.
35 MARY: Love?

1   THISTLE: I would guess you've loved Betsy Muffet
2   since you first laid eyes on her, am I right, Mr.
3   Piper?
4   *(TOM nods shyly.)*
5   BETSY: You ... you love me?
6   THISTLE: *(To TOM)* But you worked in the mail room,
7   and Ms. Muffet was the executive assistant to the
8   publisher.
9   TOM: *(To BETSY)* I ... I was going to tell you ... sometime.
10 THISTLE: Unfortunately, Ms. Muffet, you wouldn't have
11   been around long.
12 BETSY: What do you mean?
13 THISTLE: I found this in your paycheck. *(He holds up*
14   *a pink slip.)* Ms. Goose was firing you.
15 MARY: So *you* were threatening her on the phone
16   yesterday!
17 BETSY: *(Angry)* After all I'd done for her, she was
18   going to hire someone else at half the salary!
19 TOM: Don't say any more, Betsy!
20 BETSY: *(Sweetly)* So you grabbed the videotape so I
21   wouldn't be caught with it? *(TOM nods.)* You silly
22   young man. If only you'd said something ... you
23   don't know how I looked forward to getting the
24   mail every day.
25 TOM: Gosh ... you mean it?
26 JACK: Detective, now that you've got the video, you've
27   got all the evidence you need.
28 MARY: Let's watch it.
29 THISTLE: This? It's an old hockey game. Rangers
30   versus Avs, I think.
31 JENNY: What?
32 BETSY: You mean it was just a trick?
33 THISTLE: Just like the red herring about the second
34   will. What's good for the goose is good for the
35   gander. I didn't think you'd fall for it 'til I gave

1   you that call. *(In a raspy voice)* Check the box on
2   the mantel.
3 TOM: We'll get a lawyer, Ms. Muffet! I'll do everything
4   I can. They don't have any solid evidence.
5 THISTLE: Just the manager at Starbucks who's
6   willing to swear you bought a hot chocolate
7   yesterday at seven forty-two, and that you insisted
8   it be put in a plain container. And then there's the
9   store where you bought the rat poison ...
10 BOBBY: You're going to need more than one good
11   lawyer, Ms. Muffet!
12 THISTLE: Let's go.
13 TOM: Can I go along?
14 THISTLE: Who am I to squelch young love? *(THISTLE*
15   *leads BETSY and TOM Off Left.)*
16 BOBBY: Can you beat that? All a lousy trick!
17 MARY: At least they found each other.
18 JENNY: *(Sighing)* Almost like a happy ending.
19   *(DAME TROT enters Left.)*
20 DAME: Oh, dear, can anyone help me? My three little
21   kittens have lost their mittens, and they've begun
22   to cry!
23   *(The curtain falls.)*

Case of the Dangerfield Diamond

Synopsis:
In classic film noir, a tough-talking private eye is hired by a beautiful woman to solve a murder. Often narrating his thoughts to the audience, the detective finds his way through a shadowy maze of sinister characters, each of whom could have committed the crime. In this noir parody, Nick Noir has his hands full as he tries to solve a big case that just might put his name on the map.

Characters (3 male, 4 female):
NICK NOIR, private eye
DORA DANGERFIELD, daughter of the late gazillionaire,
    Dabney Dangerfield
DAPHNE DANGERFIELD, Dabney's widow
DELIA DANGERFIELD, Dabney's niece
DONALD DANGERFIELD, Dabney's nephew
CLEO CLEMDIDDLE, the Dangerfield family lawyer
BOB, the butler

Setting:
The home office of Dabney Dangerfield. Fireplace Up Center with portrait of Dabney hanging above. Desk Up Right cluttered with phone, files, and papers. Several chairs here and there. Table Down Left set with drinks and ice bucket. Window Up Left.

Props:
Cellphone; sock with darning egg, thread, and needle; legal papers and briefcase for Cleo; purses for Delia, Dora, and Daphne; briefcase for Donald; dust rag or feather duster; ice bucket with ice cubes (fake ice cubes would work best); checkbook; single glass of iced tea; tongs; tray set with six glasses of iced tea; vial; corkscrew; diamond.

Costumes:
Modern dress for all characters. Nick wears a trench coat and fedora. Bob wears a butler uniform or a dark suit.

Sound Effects:
A police siren; a cellphone ringing.

1   **Scene One**

2

3   *A street corner, played before the curtain. Night.*

4   *(AT RISE: NICK NOIR leans against proscenium. He*

5   *wears a trench coat and fedora.)*

6   **NICK:** *(To Audience)* **See that run-down building over**

7   **there? The one with the dirty green door and the**

8   **paint-chipped trim? That's where I've got my**

9   **office. It's on the second floor. The two grimy**

10   **windows right above the doorway. You can just**

11   **make out the letters on the window at the left.**

12   **Nick Noir, Private I. I had to use the letter "I"**

13   **'cause I couldn't afford to spell it out E-Y-E. Those**

14   **gold stick-on letters cost a pretty penny, and I've**

15   **never even seen a pretty penny. Two years in this**

16   **business and I was barely managing to scrape by.**

17   **All the good business went to the boys downtown,**

18   **the boys who'd got the fancy offices and the good-**

19   **looking secretaries. I had a secretary once. She**

20   **lasted a week. She ran off when she found a**

21   **mouse eating her lunch for the third time that**

22   **week. You know? If I had any brains, I'd have**

23   **given up this dream of being a private eye and**

24   **gone back to what I know best. Whatever that**

25   **was. And just when I was ready to find out, my**

26   **phone rang.** *(Phone rings. NICK pulls out his*

27   *cellphone.)* **Nick Noir, what do you want me to keep**

28   **my eye on? ... Who? ... Daphne Dangerfield?** *The*

29   **Daphne   Dangerfield?   Widow   of   Dabney**

30   **Dangerfield the gazillionaire? ... Well, say, there ...**

31   **how's it going? ... You don't say! ... You don't say!**

32   **... You don't say! I guess that says it all. Well, now,**

33   **let me check my schedule. This is my busy time of**

34   **year, after all, what with Mother's Day coming up.**

35   **You know? As a favor to you I can be at your**

1	place in half an hour. ... Take a right, then a left,
2	then a right, then a left, up a hill, take a right,
3	down a hill, take another right, then a left, and a
4	right, and I'm right there, right? *(NICK hangs up,*
5	*grinning.)* Well, I thought maybe things were
6	beginning to look up for Nick Noir. Even if my
7	horoscope said today would be filled with danger!
8	*(Lights dim to darkness.)*
9	
10	Scene Two
11	
12	*The study, three hours later.*
13	*(AT RISE: DAPHNE sits in chair darning socks.*
14	*DORA stands looking out window. DELIA paces*
15	*Downstage. DONALD sits behind desk, feet on the*
16	*papers. CLEO sits working on a legal brief. BOB dusts.)*
17	DELIA: Any sign of that idiot detective, Cousin Dora?
18	DORA: No. Wait ... wait ... that might be ... no ... it's
19	just a skunk.
20	DELIA: Aunt Daphne, you said he'd be here two and
21	a half hours ago!
22	DAPHNE: Delia, darling, maybe the traffic's awful.
23	DONALD: There's never any traffic coming up here to
24	Dangerfield Manor. Why would anyone ever come
25	up here?
26	DELIA: You should have contacted a reputable
27	detective, Aunt Daphne.
28	DAPHNE: I'm sure Mr. Noir is reputable.
29	DELIA: Has anyone you know ever used him before?
30	CLEO: Personally I always use Snoop, Snoop, and
31	Scoop. They've got a nice uptown office and a
32	secretary.
33	DONALD: I only use Smirk, Quirk, and Dirt when I
34	need to keep an eye on something ... or someone.
35	DORA: How'd you pick this one, Mommy?

1 DAPHNE: Mommy closed her eyes and said "Round
2 and round my finger goes ... where it stops,
3 nobody knows!" And then I opened my eyes and I
4 was pointing to Nick Noir. *(A door knock is heard*
5 *Off Left.)* There he is now!
6 DELIA: I hope he works faster than he drives!
7 DAPHNE: Bob, get the door, please.
8 *(BOB picks up ice bucket.)*
9 BOB: Yes, Madam!
10 DONALD: I say, Bob, you can leave the ice bucket.
11 BOB: I thought perhaps you might want it freshened
12 up. *(BOB exits Left. ALL freeze as NICK enters Right.)*
13 NICK: *(To Audience)* Only two and a half hours late, I
14 finally found Dangerfield Manor. I knocked on the
15 front door, then slipped in the back way just to
16 catch 'em off guard. I knew right away this was
17 going to be an interesting case. *(During the next part*
18 *of his speech, NICK moves to all the wrong characters.)*
19 With my vast experience, I could tell everything I
20 needed to know about these characters. *(He stands*
21 *beside DELIA.)* I knew this was Dangerfield's crusty
22 wife, a woman who'd clawed her way to
23 respectability and didn't care who she ripped up
24 in the process. *(He moves to DONALD.)* And then
25 there was Dangerfield's son. A hopeless romantic
26 who feels success is the result of hard work and
27 determination. The fool. *(He moves to DAPHNE.)*
28 And then there's Dangerfield's grandmother. They
29 say she's bumped off her share of enemies. Don't
30 let the darning socks fool you. *(He moves to DORA.)*
31 How about Dangerfield's younger sister who
32 wants nothing but the family fortune and now has
33 it. *(He moves to CLEO.)* And I don't know who this
34 is, but I wouldn't mind taking her to a karaoke
35 place some night. I'll bet she'd sing like a canary.

1   *(BOB enters with ice bucket and all return to normal.*
2   *At first no one notices NICK.)*
3   BOB: No one at the door, Mrs. Dangerfield.
4   DONALD: Well, where is that idiot?
5   NICK: Right behind you. I slipped in the back way. *(To*
6   *BOB)* And who are you?
7   BOB: Bob.
8   ALL: The butler!
9   DAPHNE: So, you must be Nick.
10   NICK: Yeah, I'm Nick. Nick Noir.
11   DELIA: What took you so long?
12   NICK: I made a second left when I should have made
13   a third right. And then I remembered, two rights
14   never make a wrong.
15   DONALD: Just be sure you don't charge us for an
16   extra two hours.
17   NICK: What do you care? Your father left you well
18   provided for!
19   DONALD: My father?
20   CLEO: He's the nephew.
21   DELIA: The classic ne'r-do-well nephew.
22   DONALD: Oh, and you're a titan of industry, sister
23   dear?
24   NICK: I thought you were the widow.
25   DAPHNE: I'm the widow.
26   NICK: Not the grandmother?
27   DORA: I'm the grandmother!
28   NICK: I gotta get out of here!
29   DORA: Just kidding! I'm the daughter.
30   DAPHNE: My precious Dora.
31   CLEO: And I'm the lawyer.
32   NICK: And I'm going bonkers!
33   CLEO: Don't. The case is very simple. We've hired you
34   to find the Dangerfield Diamond.
35   NICK: The what?

1   DONALD: You've never heard of it?
2   NICK: *(Covering)* Oh, the Dangerfield Diamond!
3   DELIA: Ten thousand luscious carats.
4   NICK: I like carrots, but I'd never call them luscious.
5   DAPHNE: She means the diamond weighs ten thousand
6   carats.
7   DORA: And it's lavender. A beautiful lavender ... like
8   a bar of soap.
9   NICK: So this diamond is missing?
10 DAPHNE: It disappeared this morning.
11 NICK: When did you see it last?
12 DAPHNE: Last night. I always wear it for dinner.
13 DORA: We can use the extra light at the dinner table.
14   Father was too cheap to use hundred-watt bulbs.
15 DAPHNE: Anyway, last night I took it off after dinner,
16   as usual, and placed it in my jewelry case.
17 NICK: Not the safe?
18 DAPHNE: Why? Only the family was here ... and Bob.
19 ALL: The butler!
20 NICK: I get the picture. Thanks.
21 DAPHNE: This morning I noticed it was gone.
22 NICK: You always look at it in the morning?
23 DAPHNE: Of course. I give it its bath.
24 NICK: You bathe your diamond?
25 DAPHNE: Why do you think it sparkles so?
26 NICK: Good point.
27 CLEO: Can you find the diamond, Nick Noir?
28 DAPHNE: It means so much to me. Dabney gave it to
29   me for our sixth ... no seventh ... maybe it was our
30   eighth anniversary ... or perhaps it was Christmas.
31 NICK: Your husband's recently deceased, as I recall.
32 DONALD: Poor Uncle Dabney.
33 DELIA: Out on the yacht for a spin around the sea.
34 DORA: And then he had that nasty fall over the back
35   of the boat.

1   DAPHNE: We tried to fend off the sharks.

2   DONALD: But they were so hungry.

3   NICK: A tragedy. But you've all managed to be consoled

4   by the fact that you ain't hurtin'.

5   CLEO: Mr. Dangerfield was most generous. He allowed

6   the estate to be divided among his wife, daughter,

7   niece, and nephew.

8   NICK: A real family affair. How about the diamond?

9   Who got that?

10   DAPHNE: I did, of course.

11   CLEO: And it's worth ten million dollars.

12   NICK: Not exactly chicken feed. But tell me this. No

13   thief on earth could fence a bauble that big. It'd

14   be like trying to sell the Mona Lisa.

15   DONALD: Not exactly, Mr. Noir. You can't cut up your

16   Mona Whoever. But you can cut up the

17   Dangerfield Diamond.

18   DELIA: And all those little diamonds could sell for ...

19   DAPHNE: What do you think, Ms. Clemdiddle?

20   CLEO: Five million, at least.

21   NICK: That's nothing to sneeze at. *(NICK sneezes loudly.)*

22   Sorry.

23   DONALD: Well, I've got an appointment I'm already

24   late for. *(He grabs his briefcase.)*

25   DELIA: *(Grabbing her purse)* Me, too!

26   DAPHNE: I'm late for the hairdresser's. *(She grabs her*

27   *purse.)*

28   DORA: *(Grabbing purse also)* I'm going to Wal-Mart to

29   pick up some cuticle remover.

30   CLEO: *(Standing, holding her briefcase)* And I'm heading

31   to court to check on some briefs.

32   *(ALL freeze but NICK.)*

33   NICK: *(To Audience)* I knew right then this case was

34   fishier than a two-week old tuna sandwich. It was

35   Sunday, and you couldn't check your briefs at

1   court on a Sunday! On top of that, every one of
2   'em had a suspicious look in their eyes, like beady
3   little red coals at the bottom of a fireplace. Trying
4   to look cool, but still hot enough to cause trouble.
5   And the way they were each clutching a purse or
6   briefcase made me wonder — what's inside that's
7   so important? But a good private eye works on
8   intuition. And mine was saying keep your eye on
9   Bob —
10   *(ALL come to life.)*
11 **ALL:** The butler!
12 **CLEO:** We trust you'll find the diamond, detective?
13 **NICK:** I'll find it ... or my name ain't Nick.
14 **ALL:** Nick Noir!
15   *(ALL exit Right and Left except for BOB and NICK.)*
16 **BOB:** Can I fetch you something, Mr. Noir?
17 **NICK:** Sure. How about some iced tea?
18 **BOB:** Very good, sir. *(BOB exits Right. NICK begins to*
19   *look around the room.)*
20 **NICK:** *(To Audience)* Taking a cue from Edgar Allan
21   Poe, I figured the diamond must be hidden in
22   plain sight. So I looked in all the logical places.
23   And then I found the Dangerfield checkbook. I
24   couldn't resist looking through it to see what
25   gazillionaires spend their money on. *(At the desk he*
26   *flips through a checkbook.)* Surprisingly, it was all
27   very mundane. Phone bills, car insurance, pool
28   maintenance, house payments *(He whistles.)* ...
29   maybe they oughta try refinancing to bring that
30   down a bit. And then I found something mighty
31   suspicious. A check for two hundred and fifty
32   thousand dollars to a Doctor Felix Fixit. Where
33   had I heard that name before?
34   *(BOB enters Right carrying a glass of tea with a few*
35   *ice cubes in it.)*

1   BOB: Here we go, sir.

2   NICK: Looks good. Thanks! *(NICK takes glass and moves*

3   *to ice bucket.)*

4   BOB: What are you doing?

5   NICK: Iced tea needs a bit more ice than this.

6   BOB: Then allow me!

7   NICK: I can do it, Bob!

8   BOB: But it's my job!

9   *(While struggling with the iced tea, BOB and NICK*

10   *knock over the ice bucket.)*

11 NICK: Oops!

12 BOB: Now look what you've done! You idiot! *(BOB is on*

13   *his hands and knees putting ice cubes back in the ice*

14   *bucket.)*

15 NICK: Say, it's just ice. I'll help you.

16 BOB: No! No! Get out! Get out of here, now!

17 NICK: *(To Audience)* Rather than get in a snit with the

18   hired help, I thought I ought to make a quick exit

19   before Bob put *me* on ice!

20   *(The curtain falls.)*

21

22   Scene Three

23

24 *A street corner, the following day. Played before the curtain.*

25   *(AT RISE: NICK leans against proscenium.)*

26 NICK: *(To Audience)* So the Case of the Dangerfield

27   Diamond was cooking up to be a stinky stew if

28   there ever was one. I knew I shoulda followed

29   each and every one of the family — and that shifty

30   lawyer to boot. But I couldn't be five places at

31   once. And I couldn't expect my secretary to do a

32   Della Street since I didn't have a secretary. And I

33   wasn't Perry Mason. But maybe it wasn't all bad.

34   By staying back at the house I found out two

35   things. One, that strange check to Doctor Felix

1	Fixit. And this morning I planned to find out what
2	that was all about. Two, Bob the butler was
3	weirder than a football bat. Why would anybody
4	get so bent out of shape over a little spilled ice?
5	And that's when it hit me! *(NICK takes out phone and*
6	*dials. Into phone)* I need the number of Dangerfield
7	Manor, please. ... What do you mean it's not listed?
8	Look, lady, this is Nick Noir, private eye. I need to
9	get in touch with the Dangerfields right now. I'm
10	working on a case for them! ... What do you mean,
11	you don't care? Stop saying "It's an unlisted
12	number"! What are you, a robot? ... Oh, you are.
13	Well, thanks for nothing. *(He puts phone away. To*
14	*Audience)* Of all the lousy luck. There oughta be a
15	law against unlisted numbers! *(He snaps his*
16	*fingers.)* Wait a second! There oughta be a *law!* *(He*
17	*takes phone out again and dials. Into phone)* Look, you
18	catatonic computer ... give me the number for Cleo
19	Clemdiddle, attorney at law. ... Five five five, one
20	two three four? Thanks! *(To Audience)* Sometimes
21	you just gotta be smarter than the computer! *(He*
22	*dials. Into phone)* Yeah, Cleo Clemdiddle, please. ...
23	Sure she knows me. This is Nick. Nick Noir. ...
24	Sure, I'll hold. ... Hey, Ms. Clemdiddle, can you do
25	me a favor? Round up the family around the
26	campfire at seven tonight in the same room we
27	were in yesterday. ... Yeah, I know who's got the
28	diamond. ... Tut, tut, you'll just have to wait and
29	see. Bye bye! *(NICK hangs up. To Audience)* I could
30	practically taste the big, fat fee that I'd get paid
31	probably on the spot. Maybe tomorrow I'd be able
32	to afford those extra letters so I could do my office
33	up right.
34	*(Lights dim to darkness.)*
35	

1   Scene Four

2

3 *The study at Dangerfield Manor, that night at eight o'clock.*

4 *(AT RISE: ALL are in the same positions as they were*

5 *at the start of Scene Two.)*

6 DELIA: I can't believe he's late again!

7 DAPHNE: He'll be here, Delia, dear.

8 DORA: And then we'll have our diamond back.

9 DONALD: You make it sound like a rattlesnake, Dora.

10 DELIA: I passed up a date with Sydney Snodgrass to

11   be here tonight.

12 DONALD: So? I passed up a date with Sydney

13   Sorrenson to be here. And she's much more

14   beautiful than your Sydney.

15 DELIA: But she's such a snob!

16 DONALD: Your Sydney's no prize! He wears a toupee!

17 DELIA: But it's an expensive toupee.

18 DORA: What if you both married Sydneys! Or better —

19   what if they married each other?! *(She laughs.)*

20 CLEO: How sweet such simple things amuse Dora so.

21 DAPHNE: She always was such an easy child.

22 DORA: *(Menacingly)* Long as I get what I want!

23   *(A door knock is heard Off Left.)*

24 DAPHNE: There he is now. Would you get the door,

25   Bob —

26 ALL: The butler!

27 BOB: Very good, Madam! *(BOB exits Left. NICK enters*

28   *Right. ALL freeze.)*

29 NICK: *(To Audience)* I scanned the room. It was just as

30   before. Except now I really had a handle on these

31   people. I knew them backwards, forwards, inside

32   out. And the picture I could paint wouldn't have

33   been very pretty.

34   *(BOB enters Left. ALL come to life.)*

35 BOB: There was no one at the door.

1   NICK: Got ya!
2   DONALD: Really, Mr. Noir! Do you always make it a
3   habit to sneak in the back way?
4   NICK: Make you nervous?
5   DELIA: Next time we'll lock the door.
6   NICK: There won't need to be a next time.
7   CLEO: That's right. You said you know who stole the
8   diamond.
9   NICK: I sure do!
10 DAPHNE: Well, who is it, Mr. Noir?
11 NICK: How about a drink first? My throat's dry as a
12   bone in Death Valley.
13 DAPHNE: In that case, drinks all around, Bob —
14 ALL: The butler!
15   *(BOB bows, exits Right.)*
16 CLEO: So, Mr. Noir, I assume the diamond is close by?
17 NICK: Indubitably!
18 DONALD: How clever of you to work so fast!
19 DORA: How'd you figure it out?
20 NICK: I just put on my thinking cap.
21 DORA: Gosh, I wish I'd had one of those in school.
22 DELIA: What did you think about?
23 NICK: Edgar Allan Poe.
24 DAPHNE: Oh, he wrote *Huckleberry Hound*, didn't he?
25 NICK: That was Mark Twain, Ma'am.
26 DAPHNE: Well, I knew it was some sort of cartoon.
27 DELIA: No, Aunt Daphne ... Poe wrote "Once upon a
28   midnight dreary, while I bathed all weak and
29   weary ..."
30 NICK: That's him. Kinda.
31 DORA: Did he play Sleepy in *Snow White?*
32 NICK: No, Poe was a genius!
33 DONALD: And what does a genius have to do with the
34   Dangerfield Diamond?
35 NICK: Poe thought the best place to hide something

1   was in plain sight.
2   *(BOB enters Right with tray of glasses holding iced tea*
3   *without any ice. He moves to table where the ice bucket*
4   *sits.)*
5   DELIA: That's the most ridiculous thing —
6   NICK: Is it? How many times have you lost something
7   and looked everywhere and then found it was
8   right under your nose all the time?
9   DAPHNE: Where is my darning egg?
10   DONALD: Aunt Daphne, it's in your lap!
11   *(DAPHNE holds up a darning egg.)*
12   NICK: You see what I mean?
13   DELIA: I suppose it's true enough.
14   *(BOB puts ice from bucket into the glasses.)*
15   NICK: So where would one want to hide a huge
16   diamond while he or she waits for the right
17   moment to smuggle it out of the house?
18   DORA: Up in a chandelier!
19   DAPHNE: How clever of you, sweetie! That's a perfect
20   place!
21   *(BOB serves the iced tea.)*
22   NICK: An excellent spot, yes.
23   DELIA: How about the bottom of a fish tank?
24   DONALD: Oh, yes! That'd be perfect mixed in with all
25   those little rocks that sparkle. No one would
26   notice a diamond.
27   NICK: You're getting very good at this.
28   CLEO: Or in the fancy rocks that one puts around the
29   base of a plant. They glow and sparkle, too!
30   DAPHNE: Why we'd all make such wonderful thieves,
31   wouldn't we?
32   DORA: Except for one thing.
33   *(We see BOB put a vial of something in the last glass*
34   *of tea, which he will serve to NICK.)*
35   DONALD: What's that, Dora?

1 DORA: We don't have a fish tank ... or a chandelier.

2 DELIA: Or a potted plant.

3 CLEO: So where is the Dangerfield Diamond?

4 BOB: Here you go, Nick ... Nick Noir ... your iced tea.

5 *(BOB hands NICK the poisoned tea.)*

6 DAPHNE: A toast, everyone! A toast to Mr. Noir for

7 being so clever! *(ALL drink except for NICK.)* What's

8 wrong, Mr. Noir?

9 BOB: Don't care for tea?

10 NICK: Au contraire, Bob. This tea is to *die* for! It's so

11 full of cyanide it could bump off a herd of

12 elephants.

13 DELIA: Cyanide?

14 DAPHNE: How horrible!

15 DONALD: Ours didn't have cyanide in them, did they?

16 NICK: No, you're all right. None of you was about to

17 accuse Bob of stealing the Dangerfield Diamond!

18 CLEO: Bob?

19 ALL: The butler?

20 NICK: Precisely!

21 DELIA: That's right! The butler always does it!

22 DAPHNE: But where is my precious baby?

23 *(BOB moves to the ice bucket.)*

24 NICK: In the ice bucket!

25 CLEO: How clever! No one but a servant would look in

26 there!

27 NICK: Why don't you fish precious out, Bob? Things

28 will go better for you!

29 CLEO: And I know a good lawyer who'll get you off

30 easy!

31 *(BOB pulls out a corkscrew.)*

32 BOB: Get back! All of you! It's mine! All mine! *(BOB*

33 *picks up the ice bucket.)*

34 DAPHNE: Why, Bob? Why?

35 BOB: Because you got everything! After all these years

166

1   of faithful service, all Mr. Dangerfield left me with
2   is a permanent job!
3 CLEO: Mr. Dangerfield thought you'd be happy. No
4   one could ever fire you no matter how many
5   dishes you broke.
6 BOB: Happy? Working for this bunch of greedy
7   vultures?
8 DAPHNE: Really, Bob, if you felt that way —
9 BOB: I figure the diamond is fine payback! *(DORA*
10   *sneaks behind BOB with a serving tray.)* I know a guy
11   who'll cut this puppy into a hundred smaller
12   diamonds, and he only wants thirty percent. That
13   ought to leave me plenty for a lifetime on the
14   beaches of paradise! Some people just dream
15   about things like that. But I'm going to live it!
16   *(DORA slams BOB in the head with tray. BOB drops*
17   *the ice bucket as he falls. DONALD, DORA, DAPHNE,*
18   *DELIA, and CLEO fall to their knees looking for the*
19   *diamond.)*
20 NICK: *(To Audience)* It was a disgusting spectacle.
21   Grown people scrambling about on the floor
22   looking for a diamond like it was an eyeball or
23   something.
24   *(Sound of police siren is heard in the distance.)*
25 DONALD: Excellent, Mr. Noir! You've even got the
26   police in on it!
27 DAPHNE: Here it is! Here it is! My precious little baby!
28   *(DAPHNE holds up a diamond the size of a golf ball.*
29   *ALL rise.)*
30 DELIA: Is it all right?
31 DAPHNE: Not a scratch on it.
32 DORA: It's good to have the whole family together
33   again.
34 CLEO: And Mr. Noir, you'll be receiving a hefty fee
35   from the family.

1   NICK: Music to my ears! But there's still a bit of
2   unfinished business.
3   CLEO: *(Nervously)* What ... what are you talking about?
4   NICK: Doctor Felix Fixit!
5   *(ALL gasp.)*
6   DONALD: What do you know about him?
7   NICK: He's the county coroner, isn't he?
8   DELIA: Not any more.
9   DAPHNE: Resigned, I think.
10 CLEO: Retired, actually.
11 DORA: He's moving to Aruba.
12 NICK: Thanks to a nice little check he received from
13   you!
14 CLEO: I think your services are no longer required,
15   Mr. Noir.
16 NICK: I think they're required more now than ever.
17 DONALD: What are you saying?
18 NICK: I'm saying you were all on the boat the day Mr.
19   Dangerfield died.
20 DAPHNE: It was a fun family outing.
21 DORA: We all loved the salt air.
22 NICK: You hated it, and you know it. Barnacle Bill at
23   the dock will testify that none of you ever liked to
24   go out with Mr. Dangerfield when he took his
25   yacht for a spin around the sea.
26 DAPHNE: Barnacle Bill the Blabbermouth!
27 DONALD: Well, Uncle Dabney was kind of a crazy
28   driver.
29 NICK: But the day he died you were all there!
30 DELIA: We wanted to bring a smile to the old boy's
31   face.
32 NICK: You wanted to bring a blunt object to his head!
33 DAPHNE: Why, that's awful! We never did such a
34   thing!
35 NICK: Sure you did! You got him way out to sea,

1   conked him on the head, dumped him overboard,

2   and then pulled him back in after he drowned.

3   DONALD: If you remember, Uncle Dabney was

4   completely eaten up by sharks.

5   NICK: Sorry, but I got the real autopsy report at my

6   office. It says Mr. Dangerfield was hit on the head

7   with a blunt object and then drowned. Nobody

8   took a bite out of him but his very greedy

9   relatives!

10   DAPHNE: How did you get your hands on that report?

11   NICK: Simple! I told Doctor Fixit to either give me the

12   real autopsy or he was going to jail!

13   DORA: But we paid him quarter of a million to lie!

14   DONALD: Shut up!

15   NICK: You can shut up anyone you like, but the whole

16   story's gonna come out, so just give it up. And

17   don't try for the corkscrew. The cops are here

18   already!

19   DELIA: *(To DAPHNE)* You just had to play "Round and

20   round the world I go!"

21   DAPHNE: You think I'm dumb as that? I phoned

22   around and asked for the most imcompetent,

23   stupid, most unprofessional private eye in the

24   business!

25   *(NICK steps in front of the curtain as it falls.)*

26   NICK: *(To Audience)* Yeah ... her words really hurt. But

27   I knew when the papers got hold of the story, I'd

28   be on top of the world. After all, not only did I get

29   the diamond back, but I caught Dabney

30   Dangerfield's murderers. That oughta be worth

31   something. Unfortunately there wasn't anybody

32   left to pay my fee for either of those two cases.

33   Still, the publicity alone would generate more

34   business than I could handle. I know I'm gonna

35   get those extra two letters. And a secretary. And

1   maybe a leather couch. All I gotta do is wait for
2   the phone to ring. *(A pause)* And it's gonna ring.
3   *(Another pause)* Any second now! *(Phone rings.)* See
4   what I mean? *(NICK answers phone.)* Nick here.
5   Nick Noir. ... Yes, Ma'am. I can find anything. ...
6   A snake? You want me to find your snake? Look,
7   lady, I don't do snakes. But wait a second. How
8   much for this snake? ... Oh, yeah? He must mean
9   a lot to you ... a whole lot. ... Oh, he swallowed
10   your poodle and you want the poodle back. Well,
11   leave it to Nick Noir! What's the address? ... A
12   right ... a left ... another right ...
13   *(Lights fade to darkness.)*

170

The Little Women Mystery

Synopsis:
A women's monthly book club would be the most unlikely place to hide a murderer, wouldn't it? But after one of the members of the Alcott Little Women's Book Club dies mysteriously, a gutsy hairdresser realizes that one member of the group has volumes to hide ... and one can never judge a book by its cover!

Characters (7 female):
GLORIA JEAN GAMBEL, 20s, a hairdresser
EDNA BALMFORTH, 50s, a retired English teacher
WILLADEAN PRICE, 30s, a poet
VAL LAWSON, 30s, a real estate agent
TERESA BRIZOLLI, 40s, a homemaker
MARGO TILLY, 20s, a graphic artist
SANDRA COLLETT, 30s, police chief

Setting:
The play takes place in the living room of Gloria Jean's house, a small bungalow in the town of Alcott. A couch Center is flanked by two mismatched chairs. A coffee table sits in front of the couch. Wing entrance Down Right leads to outside. Wing entrance Down Left leads to other rooms in the house.

Props:
Towel; drink glasses; copy of book *Who Slew the Shrew?*; cellphone; tray of cookies; copy of book *Sherlock and Me — How to Solve Any Crime*; engagement ring; piece of cake; handcuffs.

Costumes:
Modern dress for all. Sandra wears a blue police shirt along with dark pants. She can wear a hat, but it is not necessary.

Sound Effect:
Cellphone ring.

1   **Scene One**

2

3   *Late evening.*

4   *(AT RISE: EDNA sits on couch along with*

5   *WILLADEAN. MARGO sits in chair, while VAL stands*

6   *Up Right back to audience, speaking into her cellphone.*

7   *GLORIA stands Up Left wiping her shirt with a towel.*

8   *Glasses sit on coffee table along with a copy of the book*

9   Who Slew the Shrew?*)*

10 **GLORIA:** Sure hope this punch comes out!

11 **MARGO:** A little Spray 'n' Wash will take it out like

12   that! *(MARGO snaps her fingers.)*

13 **GLORIA:** I am just too clumsy for words! Every shirt I

14   got's stained with this, that, or whatever!

15 **WILLADEAN:** You ought to wear your smock at home.

16 **GLORIA:** Honey, it's my policy to never, ever bring my

17   work home with me! I don't even comb my hair at

18   home, just like I'll bet you don't ... well, you being

19   a poet and all, you probably do work at home!

20 **WILLADEAN:** To be honest, I write everywhere.

21 **EDNA:** Will the library be getting a copy of your next

22   volume, Willadean?

23 **WILLADEAN:** It's first on the list!

24 **EDNA:** So, Gloria, if you want to keep your clothes

25   clean, just try to be neater.

26 **GLORIA:** You said a mouthful, Edna, honey.

27 **EDNA:** I really wish you wouldn't call me honey.

28 **GLORIA:** Sorry! You told me that the last time we got

29   together, and here I am doin' it again! Old habits

30   die hard.

31 **EDNA:** Speaking of dying ...

32 **VAL:** *(Snapping her phone shut)* Well, of all the nerve!

33 **GLORIA:** What's wrong, Val, honey?

34 **VAL:** The Baileys backed out of the sale!

35 **MARGO:** Weren't they buying a big house in

1   Sherwood Forest?
2 VAL: Sherwood Glen. And not a big house — *the* big
3   house!
4 WILLADEAN: Your million dollar baby?
5 VAL: Gone!
6 EDNA: Probably didn't get their loan. I can't believe
7   how many people overextend themselves these
8   days! But then, everything's for show nowadays.
9   Nothing's sensible anymore.
10 VAL: They didn't overextend themselves! They found a
11   *bigger* house in Nottinghill Estates.
12 EDNA: I rest my case!
13 VAL: If I could get my hands on them, I'd ...
14 WILLADEAN: *(With a laugh)* Oh, heavens, Val, don't
15   say anything you'd be sorry for later.
16 VAL: *(Laughing)* Well, I would!
17 GLORIA: You just sit down, dear, and remember
18   tomorrow's another day.
19 EDNA: Thank you, Scarlett.
20 GLORIA: Huh?
21 EDNA: That line's from Scarlett O'Hara in *Gone With*
22   *the Wind*. Margaret Mitchell? 1936?
23 GLORIA: Oh, yeah! Before my time. Anywho ... maybe
24   we ought to get back to discussing *Who Slew the*
25   *Shrew?*
26 EDNA: I don't see why you picked that book for our
27   club, Gloria.
28 GLORIA: I thought it'd be fun!
29 VAL: I thought it was a scream! I loved the way she
30   got rid of her boss!
31 EDNA: Silly, unbelievable melodrama.
32 MARGO: Unbelievable? You don't think somebody
33   might want to get rid of her boss?
34 GLORIA: Usually it's the other way around.
35 MARGO: I mean get rid of — *(She draws her finger*

1   *across her neck.)*

2 EDNA: *(Primly)* Hardly appropriate reading for the

3   Alcott Little Women's Book Club.

4 MARGO: Oh, Edna, honestly. We don't always have to

5   read the classics.

6 EDNA: There's nothing wrong with the classics.

7 MARGO: Of course not! Even Oprah reads them. But

8   sometimes it's fun to branch out. And if you didn't

9   like *Who Slew the Shrew?*, you're going to hate the

10   book I picked for next month!

11 GLORIA: I can't wait! What'd you pick, honey?

12   *(TERESA enters Left carrying a tray of cookies.)*

13 TERESA: Anybody hungry?

14 VAL: Oh, Teresa! You're going to force five pounds on

15   us all!

16 MARGO: What have we got this time? Cannolis?

17   Tiramisu?

18 GLORIA: Cookies!

19 TERESA: My mother's special recipes!

20 WILLADEAN: They look wonderful!

21 TERESA: And the best part — they're all fat free!

22   *(The ladies dig in.)*

23 GLORIA: I move Teresa brings the snack every time

24   we meet!

25 MARGO: I second the motion!

26 VAL: We don't even have to ask who slew the shrew —

27   she died from clogged arteries!

28 GLORIA: Did you honestly hate the book, Edna?

29 EDNA: Oh, Gloria, it's just not my type of book.

30 WILLADEAN: Then it broadens our horizons.

31 GLORIA: Well said, honey!

32 EDNA: My horizons are broad enough!

33 VAL: Who are you kidding, Edna? You were born in

34   Alcott, went to school at Alcott College, then

35   taught for two hundred years at Alcott High.

1   EDNA: Two hundred! Why, Val Lawson, I'd send you
2   to another detention if I could! *(ALL laugh.)* Well, I
3   would!
4   VAL: *(Taking EDNA's hand)* What would I have done
5   without you badgering me all the time about my
6   comma fault? I'd never have been able to write a
7   decent contract.
8   GLORIA: I guess I shouldn't have cut class so often.
9   WILLADEAN: Maybe you'd be a CEO right now.
10 GLORIA: *(Proudly)* I am a CEO ... of Waves of Glory
11   Beauty Salon.
12 WILLADEAN: I meant a rich CEO.
13 GLORIA: *(Sighing, lovingly)* Who needs rich? I got
14   Freddy.
15 MARGO: You ever gonna marry him?
16 GLORIA: Soon as he asks me.
17 VAL: You just got to light a fire under him.
18 GLORIA: Honey, I've tried everything but charcoal
19   and lighter fluid, and he's still happy to just come
20   over, sit on the couch, and watch TV with me.
21 WILLADEAN: Sounds like you're married already.
22   *(VAL'S phone rings.)*
23 VAL: *(Rising to answer it)* Val Lawson here ... oh, yes,
24   Mr. Bailey. ... Yes? ... Oh, really? I didn't know
25   that. ... All right, I certainly can. ... Fifteen
26   minutes? ... I'll see you then. Thank you.
27 MARGO: Your million dollar baby has been
28   resuscitated?
29 VAL: And how! They found out the bigger house is in
30   a different township where the property taxes are
31   twice as high.
32 EDNA: Sanity wins out!
33 VAL: I've got to run and get them to sign on the dotted
34   line before they change their minds again. What
35   are we reading next time, Margo?

1   MARGO: *(Pulling book from her purse)* **Sherlock and Me**
2   — *How to Solve Any Crime.* I think it was written
3   by somebody named Culpepper. *(She looks at the*
4   *book.)* Ooops! Was I way off. It's written by I. C.
5   Aull. I. C. Aull ... now isn't that just the funniest
6   pen name you've ever heard?
7   EDNA: Oh, goodness, Margo! Next we'll be reading
8   cookbooks!
9   TERESA: *(Thinking)* I think that might be fun!
10 GLORIA: Sounds like Sherlock will get us to exercise
11   our minds a bit.
12 MARGO: It certainly will ... and at our next meeting,
13   I'll show you just what I mean about solving a
14   crime! Even one that happened a long time ago!
15   *(The curtain falls.)*
16
17   Scene Two
18
19 *A month later.*
20   *(AT RISE: EDNA sits in the same spot, as does*
21   *WILLADEAN. TERESA sits in chair Left, while VAL*
22   *sits in chair Right. GLORIA stands Upstage wiping her*
23   *shirt with a towel.)*
24 WILLADEAN: **Déjà vu.**
25 GLORIA: You can say that again, honey.
26 TERESA: Except ... poor Margo.
27 EDNA: Hard to believe just last month she was sitting
28   there.
29 VAL : She said something about my million dollar baby
30   being resuscitated ... if only ... if only they could
31   have ...
32   *(GLORIA sits on edge of VAL's chair.)*
33 GLORIA: Oh, honey ... I'm sure they did all they could.
34   She fell down a heck of a lot of stairs.
35 WILLADEAN: I've always hated that stairway.

1 EDNA: It saves a very long walk around the hill. One
2   just has to be careful. Very careful.
3 WILLADEAN: I know, but it gets so dangerous when
4   it's icy out.
5 TERESA: There wasn't any ice that night.
6 VAL: It was almost balmy when I left. Mr. Bailey didn't
7   even have a jacket on when we went to look at the
8   house again.
9 GLORIA: They did buy it, then?
10 VAL: Yeah ... but when I heard about Margo ... well ...
11 EDNA: It didn't seem quite as important, did it?
12   *(VAL shakes her head.)*
13 TERESA: I'm just sorry that the funeral was so far
14   away.
15 GLORIA: Well, she'd just moved here from New York,
16   so it stood to reason her family'd want her back
17   where she came from.
18 TERESA: I know, but none of us was able to go.
19 WILLADEAN: And she *was* part of our club.
20 EDNA: We sent flowers.
21 GLORIA: That's right! And I wrote her family a real
22   nice letter telling 'em all about how Margo liked to
23   read and discuss.
24 TERESA: Did they write you back?
25 GLORIA: You know something funny? My letter came
26   back labeled "no such address." I'm sure it was
27   the address Margo gave me one time.
28 EDNA: Well, at least you tried, Gloria.
29 GLORIA: Did the flowers get delivered?
30 EDNA: I had them sent to a funeral home in Brooklyn.
31 GLORIA: Well, I'm sure you picked out some real
32   pretty ones, honey ... I mean Edna.
33 EDNA: Lilies and chrysanthemums. Appropriately
34   funereal.
35 VAL: Al sent me those on our first wedding

```
1        anniversary. I should have guessed the marriage
2        was in trouble!
3        (ALL laugh weakly.)
4   GLORIA: Well, now, since we're all here and this is the
5        Alcott Little Women's Book Club, did anybody
6        read Margo's selection for this meeting? Sherlock
7        and Me — How to Solve Any Crime?
8   EDNA: Oh, Gloria! Honestly, how can you bring that
9        book up now?
10  GLORIA: It's our book of the month.
11  EDNA: It's insensitive of you.
12  GLORIA: But there wasn't a crime involving Margo ...
13       (Ominously) was there?
14  VAL: Of course not!
15  WILLADEAN: It said it was an accident in the papers.
16  TERESA: She tripped and fell.
17  VAL: Easy to do with the shoes she was wearing.
18  WILLADEAN: And if she was carrying anything ...
19  EDNA: She had her purse, that's all. And she left the
20       book here, so it couldn't have been too heavy. It
21       was just an accident ... a terrible, tragic accident.
22  GLORIA: We all sound real sure about that.
23  TERESA: Gloria, what's this about?
24  GLORIA: I didn't like it when I got that letter I sent to
25       her family back. I didn't like it one bit.
26  WILLADEAN: It happens. Maybe you got the wrong
27       address.
28  GLORIA: That's what I thought. But then I looked in
29       my address book and I'd taped in the address
30       Margo had written down for me.
31  VAL: She could have gotten it wrong.
32  EDNA: Why'd you have her family's address anyway?
33  GLORIA: I knew she didn't have anybody close in
34       town and asked her one day ... you know ... just
35       in case ... somebody ought to know how to get in
```

1   touch with her family ...
2 WILLADEAN: That is so ghoulish!
3 GLORIA: Practical, if you ask me. Anywho, she wrote
4   it down, and I taped it right into my address book.
5   No point copying it over.
6 TERESA: All right ... so what does all this mean?
7 *(GLORIA picks up the book about crime.)*
8 GLORIA: I got to thinking as I paged through this here
9   book ... Margo picked it for a real special reason.
10   She didn't want us to read it as much as she
11   wanted to solve some kind of crime.
12 VAL: What kind of crime?
13 EDNA: You've seen too many movies, my dear.
14 GLORIA: If I can't call you honey, you can't call me
15   "my dear."
16 EDNA: My goodness, Gloria ... you're pretty edgy
17   tonight ...
18 GLORIA: I know ... I'm sorry ... but I couldn't help
19   remembering Margo's last words to the group:
20   "Next meeting I'll show you just what I mean
21   about solving a crime. Even one that happened a
22   long time ago!"
23   *(ALL look at one another.)*
24 TERESA: Oh, this is silly! It was just a ... what?
25 EDNA: Metaphor.
26 TERESA: Thank you.
27 GLORIA: I think she meant exactly what she said, no
28   metaphor intended.
29 VAL: Well, maybe there was some crime she knew
30   about.
31 WILLADEAN: Then she would have gone to the police.
32 GLORIA: Unless it involved one of us.
33 TERESA: *(Laughing weakly)* Us? My only crime is
34   burning the biscotti once in a while!
35 EDNA: *(Primly)* I've never even done that.

179

1   VAL: Gloria, your imagination's taking over.
2   GLORIA: Yeah, I thought so too until I went to New
3   York.
4   WILLADEAN: You ... you went to New York?
5   GLORIA: I twisted Freddy's arm, and he drove me. It
6   was that week we were closed.
7   VAL: I thought you were having the floors redone.
8   GLORIA: I lied. I just threw a couple of new rugs on
9   the floor and nobody noticed.
10 TERESA: What'd you do in New York?
11 GLORIA: *(Enjoying the memories)* Walked across the
12   Brooklyn Bridge. My, that was a beautiful sight!
13   And we went to South Street Seaport so Freddy
14   could go on those ships with all the sails ... and
15   we went to Chinatown and had real wonton soup
16   ... and I got to see Radio City Music Hall ...
17 EDNA: Gloria! What about Margo?
18 GLORIA: Oh, yeah ... So I went to the address she
19   gave me.
20 WILLADEAN: And?
21 GLORIA: It was a detective agency. The Sloane
22   Detective Agency on East Fourth Street. That's in
23   Manhattan.
24 VAL: A detective agency?
25 GLORIA: Just like in the movies.
26 EDNA: Why ... why would she have given you the
27   address of a detective agency?
28 GLORIA: Because Margo was a detective. She was
29   working a case right here in Alcott.
30 WILLADEAN: Oh, my goodness!
31 GLORIA: At least this is where it led. I talked to Mr.
32   Sloane himself, but he wouldn't tell me much at
33   all. He just said that since the coroner listed
34   Margo's death as an accident, he didn't have
35   anything much to say. He wanted to protect her

1   family, you see.

2   TERESA: So you think that's what she meant about

3   solving a crime at this meeting?

4   GLORIA: I *know* that's what she meant. Now in

5   Chapter One of the book —

6   EDNA: Gloria, you're not serious!

7   GLORIA: Dead serious, Edna. In Chapter One the

8   author talks about motive. Whoever pushed Margo

9   down those stairs had a reason for doing it.

10   VAL: *(Standing)* Look, I'm not listening to this any

11   more. I've got to get over to the Kramers anyway

12   and discuss a few things with them about their

13   sale.

14   GLORIA: *(Blocking VAL's exit)* Oh, I forgot to tell you,

15   Mr. Kramer called and said they can't meet

16   tonight. Your cell must be dead.

17   VAL: That's ridiculous! My cell is never dead! *(VAL*

18   *pulls her phone out. It's dead.)* First time for

19   everything. *(VAL relaxes, returns to party in spirit.)*

20   GLORIA: I got to thinking why anybody would want

21   to kill Margo. Now, knowing she was a detective,

22   there's one big reason — to keep her from talking.

23   Somebody hired her to find out something, and

24   she must have found it out, and whoever it was

25   about knew she found it out.

26   WILLADEAN: Gloria, that's just a book. It's probably

27   all fiction! And your imagination's working

28   overtime here.

29   TERESA: Really. This is crazy! I hope you don't think

30   one of us would do such a thing to Margo!

31   GLORIA: I think when she said she'd show us how to

32   solve a crime, she was saying that right to one of

33   us. Problem is ... which one?

34   EDNA: I don't believe this, Gloria! Not a word of it!

35   VAL: You've been sniffin' those hairdressing fumes for

1   too many years, kiddo, and your brain's going
2   fuzzy!
3   GLORIA: Since I went to New York, I wish I hadn't
4   gone. I mean ... seein' Times Square was just fine,
5   but I came back and realized just how much I
6   don't know about some of the people I like the
7   most.
8   TERESA: You know something else, too, don't you?
9   GLORIA: 'Course I do. I wouldn't bring all this up if I
10   didn't know something else.
11   VAL: So? What is it?
12   GLORIA: When I left Mr. Sloane's office, I walked into
13   the waiting room to meet Freddy 'cause he was
14   sitting there reading *Car and Driver* magazine. And
15   I looked at the cover of the magazine and there
16   was an article on some NASCAR driver named
17   Sammy Salt.
18   EDNA: Gloria, what is your point?
19   GLORIA: I'm gettin' to that!
20   VAL: I don't even know a Sammy Salt, so I'm innocent.
21   GLORIA: Oh, nothing happened to Sammy Salt. But
22   his last name jogged this old brain of mine.
23   TERESA: Can you jog it a bit faster? I got cassata cake
24   in the refrigerator.
25   GLORIA: It'll keep.
26   TERESA: But my appetite won't!
27   GLORIA: All right, all right! Salt made me think of
28   pepper —
29   VAL: *(Sarcastically)* You got that from your therapist,
30   right? Word association.
31   WILLADEAN: Let her finish, or we'll never get to the
32   cake, Val!
33   GLORIA: Thank you, Willadean. I'm glad somebody
34   here has manners. So, where was I?
35   TERESA: Salt and pepper.

1   GLORIA: That's right! Remember when Margo showed
2   us this book? At first she said it was by somebody
3   named Culpepper. That might have been a
4   mistake ... just an honest mistake, but I think it
5   was a warning to somebody in this room. I mean,
6   who'd ever forget the real name of the author, I.C.
7   Aull? So ... I turned to the receptionist —
8   VAL: What receptionist?
9   GLORIA: The one at the detective agency!
10 VAL: Oh, we're still in the waiting room. Waiting,
11   waiting, waiting.
12 GLORIA: I said to the receptionist, "I'm so glad we
13   stopped. Ms. Culpepper will be relieved after I
14   talk to her." And the receptionist smiled a bit and
15   said "It's certainly been hard for her and the rest
16   of J.J.'s family all these years. They are really
17   pinning their hopes on us." Well, the sirens and
18   whistles went off!
19 WILLADEAN: The building caught fire?
20 GLORIA: In my head! So I dragged Freddy to the New
21   York City Public Library and, my goodness, I've
22   never seen so many books in all my born days!
23 WILLADEAN: What could you learn in the library?
24 GLORIA: That's just what Chapter Two of the book
25   covers. Researching the background of a crime.
26   All I had to do was give those sweet library people
27   the name Culpepper and they brought me out a
28   whole bunch of stuff on a fellow named J.J.
29   Culpepper.
30 EDNA: And who, pray tell, is J.J. Culpepper?
31 GLORIA: Was, Edna. He's a was.
32 WILLADEAN: Who was he?
33 GLORIA: A gazillionaire! Well, at least a millionaire
34   with assets here, there, and everywhere.
35 TERESA: Never bought a cannoli from me!

1   GLORIA: And won't. He's dead. And guess how he
2   died! He fell down a long flight of stairs.
3   VAL: What?
4   GLORIA: It was ruled accidental, but the coroner
5   found a bruise on his right shoulder blade, and the
6   family thinks that he was pushed. That was back
7   eight years ago, and they've hired one detective
8   after another until Margo ...
9   EDNA: Hold it! Hold it! Do you know what you're
10   saying, my dear?
11   GLORIA: I sure do, honey. Margo found J.J.
12   Culpepper's killer in this room. And she's sitting
13   here right now.
14   VAL: That's ... that's ridiculous!
15   TERESA: *(Frightened)* One of us —
16   WILLADEAN: Gloria, you're making quite a leap here ...
17   GLORIA: I wish I was, honey, but facts are facts.
18   EDNA: What facts?
19   GLORIA: Chapter Three of the book talks about
20   modus operandi. You know what that means?
21   VAL: The M.O. How the guy does it.
22   GLORIA: Yeah ... well, we see the modus operandi is
23   the same. J.J. and Margo were pushed down stairs
24   so it would look like an accident.
25   WILLADEAN: But they probably *were* accidents!
26   GLORIA: The bruise says otherwise, honey ... and is it
27   just a coincidence they died the same way? I don't
28   think so! And then there's Margo's blurtin' out the
29   Culpepper name ... and her promise to solve the
30   crime at this meeting ... and then there was that
31   other comment she made ... about getting rid of
32   your boss.
33   TERESA: Did she say that?
34   GLORIA: You were getting the cookies, Teresa. But yes,
35   she and Edna had a bit of a discussion about that.

1 EDNA: I still say nonsense!
2 GLORIA: But it isn't! J.J. Culpepper left a million
3   dollars to his secretary, Blanche Devereau. Except
4   that the day he died, he fired Blanche Devereau
5   and called his lawyer wanting to change his will.
6   Well, J.J. never did get to change the will and so
7   Blanche got her million dollars, then vanished.
8 WILLADEAN: That doesn't mean she ... she murdered
9   him.
10 GLORIA: Apparently Blanche had been skimming a
11   bit of money out of petty cash, and J.J. found out.
12   And you can imagine his petty cash wasn't enough
13   to buy just candy bars.
14 VAL: So one of us is this Blanche Devereau?
15 GLORIA: It's not me! I can tell you that right now. I'm
16   Gloria Gambel ... soon to be Schwartz! *(GLORIA*
17   *puts on an engagement ring.)*
18 VAL: Freddy proposed?
19 GLORIA: At the top of the Empire State Building!
20 TERESA: Just like *Sleepless in Seattle*!
21 EDNA: Congratulations, Gloria! Freddy's just like a
22   tuna, and I knew you'd eventually hook him.
23 WILLADEAN: When's the wedding?
24 GLORIA: Well, it's not going to be anything big, but
25   you're all invited ... 'cept that one of you won't be
26   able to attend.
27 VAL: Oh, Gloria, stop it right now!
28 TERESA: Who's this Blanche lady?
29 GLORIA: I called the Culpeppers, and they were so
30   sweet, especially about Margo. They're donating
31   five thousand dollars to the scholarship fund we
32   set up in Margo's name ... but anyway, they said
33   that Blanche Devereau has a tattoo on her left
34   shoulder, a tattoo of a pit bull in honor of her dog,
35   Spike, who bit three people and had to be put

1   down. Ladies?
2   VAL: What?
3   GLORIA: Let's see the back of your shoulders.
4   EDNA: You think I have a tattoo? Really, my dear —
5   GLORIA: Humor me, honey!
6   EDNA: *(Baring her shoulder quickly)* There! Satisfied?
7   TERESA: I'd never get a tattoo, either! Hurts too
8   much. *(Baring her shoulder)* Just a couple of
9   freckles, right?
10 VAL: *(Baring her shoulder)* I hate dogs ... but I do have
11   a rose.
12 GLORIA: Isn't that cute!
13 EDNA: Willadean, please prove Gloria's way off base
14   so we can get on with dessert!
15 GLORIA: Willadean? You came to town seven years
16   ago, didn't you? Right after you collected your
17   million dollars. Margo's hints were directed at you,
18   weren't they? I guess she was just trying to flush
19   you out, but you followed her that night and
20   pushed her down the stairs.
21 EDNA: Willadean? That's ridiculous! She's a poet!
22 WILLADEAN: Really! I ... I've never been so insulted,
23   Gloria!
24 GLORIA: Well, now, the police did find an earring at
25   the scene of Margo's death. Just one ...
26 WILLADEAN: So?
27 GLORIA: It was one of yours. You wore them that
28   night.
29 WILLADEAN: So? I walk that way sometimes! It could
30   have fallen out of my ear by accident.
31 GLORIA: It was in Margo's hand.
32   *(WILLADEAN races Left, but bumps into police officer*
33   *SANDRA who's eating a piece of cake.)*
34 SANDRA: This is great cake, Teresa!
35 TERESA: Thank you ... Officer.

1   GLORIA: Chapter Four says to make sure the police
2   are involved. Did you get all that, Sandra?
3   SANDRA: And more. Margo left a few notes at her
4   place. But I don't remember anything about an
5   earring, Gloria.
6   GLORIA: Oh, that was in Chapter Five. If all else fails,
7   lay a trap.
8   WILLADEAN: You don't have anything! You can't
9   prove I did a thing!
10 SANDRA: But we're sure going to try. Thanks for the
11   cake! *(She cuffs WILLADEAN.)*
12 GLORIA: If you want to join the Little Women's Book
13   Club, Sandra, just let me know! We have the best
14   snacks in town.
15 SANDRA: I'll think about it. What're you reading next?
16 EDNA: Teresa?
17 TERESA: A cookbook! *Recipes to Die For!*
18   *(The curtain falls.)*

Into Thin Heir

Synopsis:
An unlikely detective is hired to find a missing — and presumed dead — heir to the Hawkthorne fortune. What she finds is a nest of vultures.

Characters (4 male, 5 female):
POLLY PEABODY, 60s, an amateur sleuth
LOLA LANE, 20s, Tewksbury Hawkthorne's niece
SYLVIA STARK, 20s, secretary to Tewksbury Hawkthorne
PHIL POTTS, 40s, Hawkthorne's attorney
NORMAN NEWCOMB, 40s, Hawkthorne's business partner
DANIELLE DEFOE, 20s, Hawkthorne's biographer
CONSTANCE BASHING, 30s, Hawkthorne's latest flame
BUTTLES, the butler
ARCHIE ADAMS, 20s, a thug

Setting:
The Great Room at Hawkthorne Manor. Wing entrance Down Right leads to main entrance and outside. Wing entrance Down Left leads to other rooms in the house. Several chairs form a group at Center. Other chairs dot the room. Fireplace Up Right. Portrait of dour old man, Tewksbury Hawkthrone, hangs Up Center. Small table Up Left.

Props:
Notebook; laptop; drink glasses; large knitting bag; silver serving tray; ice bag; official papers such as a birth certificate, rental car receipt, formal letter, etc.; metallic-looking canister; frying pan or wine bottle.

Costumes:
Modern dress for all characters. Polly should wear a somewhat dated dress. Constance dresses very lavishly with a string of huge pearls. Sylvia dresses simply. Buttles wears a butler's uniform or a suit with a bow tie. Archie wears a long coat or cape and wears a ski mask when we first see him.

1   **Scene One**

2

3   *The entrance of Tewksbury Manor, played before the curtain,*

4   *evening.*

5   *(AT RISE: A gentle knocking is heard Off Right.*

6   *BUTTLES enters Left, crossing to Right. POLLY*

7   *PEABODY enters Right, flustered. She carries a large*

8   *knitting bag.)*

9   POLLY: Oh, dear! I'm sorry to barge in, but the door

10   was open, and I thought, perhaps, nobody could

11   hear me knocking.

12   BUTTLES: Who are you, Madam?

13   POLLY: Mrs. Peabody. And you must be Buttles, the

14   butler. I've learned so much about you.

15   *(LOLA enters Left.)*

16   LOLA: Who is it, Buttles?

17   BUTTLES: Some nosy parker named Mrs. Peapod.

18   POLLY: Mrs. Peabody. And I'm not really a nosy

19   parker. I mean, I've been employed —

20   LOLA: *(With a laugh)* Take a hike, Buttles. Go freshen

21   up the drinks or something.

22   BUTTLES: Very good, Ms. Lane. *(BUTTLES bows, moves*

23   *Left, casts a glance back at MRS. PEABODY, sniffs,*

24   *exits Left.)*

25   POLLY: He doesn't take kindly to strangers, does he?

26   LOLA: He's like an old watchdog, Mrs. Peabody. But

27   his bark is worse than his bite.

28   *(Burst of laughter Off Left)*

29   POLLY: Oh, my, I'm afraid I've come at a bad time.

30   LOLA: We're just having an anniversary dinner. It's

31   been exactly one year since Uncle Tewky died and

32   we all thought we'd get together to remember him.

33   Fondly.

34   POLLY: Well, isn't this perfect timing!

35   LOLA: What ... what do you mean?

1   POLLY: I've finished my job for you.
2   LOLA: Then ... then I guess there's no hope.
3   POLLY: On the contrary! I've found your uncle's
4   missing heir.
5   *(Blackout.)*
6
7   **Scene Two**
8
9   *The Great Room, a few minutes later.*
10   *(AT RISE: POLLY stands Left Center. SYLVIA sits*
11   *Down Left, her notebook open. LOLA stands Right*
12   *Center. PHIL and NORMAN sit in chairs Center.*
13   *CONSTANCE sits Down Right nervously playing with*
14   *her pearls. DANIELLE sits Up Right using her laptop.)*
15   PHIL: So, let's get this straight, Lola ...
16   NORMAN: You hired this grandma to find J.J.
17   Hawkthorne?
18   CONSTANCE: Whatever possessed you, darling?
19   LOLA: The little matter of Uncle Tewky's fortune.
20   DANIELLE: Oh, that's not such a little matter, Ms.
21   Lane. Your uncle's fortune at the time of his death
22   was estimated at two billion dollars, and due to his
23   wise investments near the end of his life, the
24   amount has grown over the past year to two point
25   four billion. That's in U.S. dollars.
26   NORMAN: Aren't you done with that biography yet,
27   Danielle?
28   CONSTANCE: Norman, darling, she wants her share of
29   the fortune, doesn't she? The longer she can hang
30   around here typing away, the more she'll earn,
31   right, Ms. DeFoe?
32   DANIELLE: *(Defensively)* I simply want to write an
33   accurate and complete biography as Mr.
34   Hawkthorne wished.
35   PHIL: Of course, according to Mrs. Peapod here —

1   POLLY: Peabody.

2   PHIL: J.J. has been found, right?

3   POLLY: Absolutely.

4   NORMAN: As in ... no mistake?

5   CONSTANCE: Not even the slightest chance it's not

6   J.J.? *(POLLY shakes her head.)* **Drat!**

7   NORMAN: Well, Lola, you've done it this time.

8   LOLA: Well, Norman, after all, Uncle Tewky did leave

9   everything to J.J.

10 CONSTANCE: Which was a lousy thing to do to the

11   rest of us!

12 PHIL: *(With a cynical laugh)* We'll all muddle through.

13   Isn't that what the will said?

14 SYLVIA: Not exactly, Mr. Potts.

15 PHIL: I almost forgot you were here, Ms. Stark.

16   Hawkthorne's terribly efficient secretary. What,

17   exactly, did the will say?

18 SYLVIA: *(Reading from notebook)* "I leave the rest of

19   you my best wishes for a long and healthy life,

20   knowing full well you are capable of making your

21   own ends meet without any help from me.

22   Constance, I'm sure you will find someone else to

23   take care of you."

24 CONSTANCE: *(Bitterly)* Not with the money you had,

25   Tewky, my love!

26 SYLVIA: "Norman, you'll find a new partner to help

27   you run your own business into the ground."

28 NORMAN: What a rotten accusation!

29 SYLVIA: "Phillip, you have stolen so much money

30   from me you've already spent your legacy."

31 PHIL: I never took a dime I didn't deserve!

32 SYLVIA: "And Danielle, you'll make your money off

33   that book — if you ever get it done."

34 DANIELLE: So I've suffered from writer's block.

35 SYLVIA: "Lola, you'll be able to live in the house

1   because I'm sure J.J. isn't the kind of person to
2   toss you out into the cold wearing only your
3   chinchilla coat."
4 LOLA: That doesn't exactly keep me in Chanel, Uncle
5   Tewky!
6 SYLVIA: "Buttles, you can keep your job as long as
7   you like, regardless of how many drinks you spill."
8   *(BUTTLES spills a drink.)*
9 BUTTLES: Dang!
10 POLLY: And what does it say about you, Ms. Stark?
11 SYLVIA: Oh, I'm nothing but the secretary, Ms.
12   Peabody. Mr. Hawkthorne didn't include the help
13   in his will. Goodness, I didn't even know him long.
14 LOLA: So, Ms. Peabody, perhaps you ought to tell us
15   where J.J. is hiding.
16 PHIL: We deserve a look at him!
17 POLLY: In due time, Mr. Potts.
18 CONSTANCE: *(Moving to POLLY)* You know what I
19   think, doll face? I think you're lying.
20 DANIELLE: *Moi aussi!* That's French.
21 POLLY: Why would I lie?
22 PHIL: To get whatever Lola here is paying you.
23 SYLVIA: It is a known fact that J.J. Hawkthorne
24   disappeared one year ago tonight.
25 POLLY: *(Sadly, shaking her head)* The night his uncle
26   died. He was due here at the Manor, wasn't he?
27 LOLA: Yes. If everything had gone right, he would
28   have been here at nine o'clock.
29 POLLY: And he was coming from Europe, I believe?
30 CONSTANCE: Tewky felt it would be better to send
31   J.J. out of the country to be educated.
32 PHIL: Considering his life here would have been a
33   series of bad influences. *(PHIL glances at the others.)*
34 LOLA: Meaning us, of course.
35 NORMAN: Tewky never let us near the boy.

1   POLLY: Didn't any of you go over to Europe to see J.J.
2   over the years?
3   CONSTANCE: Really, Ms. Whatever, we had better
4   things to do than that!
5   DANIELLE: Besides, Mr. Hawkthorne was very
6   secretive about what schools J.J. attended. In fact,
7   he wouldn't even tell me for the biography.
8   PHIL: I think one was in Belgium.
9   CONSTANCE: No, Phillip. As always, you're wrong,
10   darling. It was Belarus.
11   NORMAN: *(With a laugh)* Belarus? They don't even
12   have schools there. It was Bulgaria!
13   POLLY: You're all wrong, I'm afraid. It was
14   Switzerland.
15   NORMAN: No, no, no! It began with a B.
16   POLLY: The Beaupres Academy in Bern.
17   CONSTANCE: Well, aren't you clever finding that out?
18   LOLA: What's your secret?
19   POLLY: I asked Ms. Stark.
20   PHIL: The secretary?
21   CONSTANCE: *(To SYLVIA)* He confided in you?
22   SYLVIA: Oh, no! I wouldn't say he confided. He just
23   asked me to make arrangements so J.J. could fly
24   back last year. He wanted to see his son one last
25   time before ... well ... before.
26   NORMAN: Couldn't J.J. have made his own
27   arrangements?
28   DANIELLE: *(Checking her notes)* He was twenty-two,
29   after all, born October twenty-second, location
30   undisclosed.
31   POLLY: It seems Mr. Hawkthorne would have gone to
32   any lengths to protect J.J.
33   LOLA: That kid was all he thought of.
34   PHIL: But ... it obviously didn't work!
35   POLLY: J.J. did pick up a rental car that night after

1   flying into JFK.
2 DANIELLE: *(Again, checking her notes)* A compact so he
3   wouldn't look conspicuous. The rental agency
4   confirmed the car was rented at eight-ten p.m.,
5   approximately one hour after his flight landed.
6 SYLVIA: His flight from Bern. SwissAir, flight ninety-
7   five.
8 POLLY: That's right. And the flight actually came in
9   fifteen minutes early. He must have passed
10   through customs quickly and had all his luggage
11   with him. No bags were left behind.
12 LOLA: Then he drove here.
13 NORMAN: But unfortunately the road got icy. It does
14   that at that time of year.
15 DANIELLE: The weather service said there was a
16   freezing drizzle that night.
17 CONSTANCE: *(She's heard it before.)* The car slid on the
18   Passaquattic Bridge and fell in. End of story.
19 POLLY: But they never found the body.
20 NORMAN: It was washed out to sea. The river was
21   running high because of all the rain, Mrs. Peapot.
22 POLLY: Peabody.
23 LOLA: Besides, no one could have survived for very
24   long in those frigid waters.
25 POLLY: Did Mr. Hawkthorne know of J.J.'s fate before
26   he, himself, died that night?
27 CONSTANCE: *(With a glance at LOLA)* Unfortunately
28   some people couldn't keep their big mouths shut!
29 LOLA: It was an accident, Constance! I've told you! I
30   never meant for him to overhear that phone call.
31 PHIL: Oh, Lola, you yapped loud enough to scare a
32   herd of elephants out of the jungle!
33 POLLY: Who were you talking to, Ms. Lane?
34 LOLA: Some reporter. I forget the name.
35 PHIL: Can you imagine the insensitivity? Well, poor old

1   Tewky died immediately, didn't he, Sylvia?

2   POLLY: You were with him when he died, Ms. Stark?

3   SYLVIA: Yes, well ... he had asked for me to come in.

4   CONSTANCE: I still can't believe that!

5   SYLVIA: Buttles knows it's the truth.

6   POLLY: Is it true, Buttles?

7   BUTTLES: Mr. Hawkthorne expressly asked that I

8   send Ms. Stark and Ms. Stark only into the room.

9   He said he wished to dictate a letter. *(BUTTLES*

10   *exits Left.)*

11   POLLY: A letter? What was in the letter?

12   SYLVIA: *(Nervously)* I ... I don't remember.

13   LOLA: Ha!

14   SYLVIA: I don't! I don't even remember writing

15   anything. I just remember ... voices.

16   POLLY: You mean Ms. Lane? *(SYLVIA nods.)* What was

17   she saying?

18   SYLVIA: The door was slightly open, and she was in

19   the hall on her cellphone. She said "My God! J.J.'s

20   dead! He's been killed in a car crash!"

21   POLLY: And that's when Mr. Hawkthorne died?

22   *(SYLVIA nods.)* I see. You've all confirmed

23   everything in the police reports, then.

24   LOLA: *(With a laugh)* You think we're lying?

25   POLLY: Oh, of course not, Ms. Lane. But it's always

26   best to start at the beginning. The basic facts are

27   simple: Mr. Hawkthorne had one child, J.J. He

28   sent the child to Europe for schooling, ostensibly

29   to protect the child from publicity —

30   NORMAN: And us.

31   POLLY: I'm sure not *all* of you. At any rate, in his will,

32   he left his entire fortune to J.J. Hawkthorne and

33   when he knew he was dying, he asked J.J. to fly

34   home from Switzerland so they could meet one

35   last time.

1 CONSTANCE: But poor J.J. got himself killed along
2   the way. *(Emphatically)* End of story.
3 PHIL: The will is now in probate because there were
4   no residual legatees mentioned.
5 LOLA: I, of course, am the only living relative —
6 CONSTANCE: But I was his ... well ... he and I had a
7   good thing going!
8 PHIL: He certainly owed me money for the legal work
9   I was completing at the time.
10 NORMAN: And I'm a quarter owner in Hawkthorne
11   Industries, which means I'm entitled to my share!
12 DANIELLE: Don't forget the biography he hired me to
13   write. I only got a small advance, and my contract
14   says I'm to be paid one million dollars upon
15   completion.
16 POLLY: Oh, dear! J.J.'s death really complicated
17   everything. But since I've found J.J., it's all very
18   simple. The Hawkthorne fortune goes to J.J., and
19   you can discuss you requests with the designated
20   heir once the paperwork is completed.
21 NORMAN: You really think you've found J.J.?
22 POLLY: Of course I did.
23 CONSTANCE: Look, lady, I hate to be brutally honest —
24 LOLA: Since when, Constance?
25 CONSTANCE: *(Smirking at LOLA)* — But how could you
26   find anything? You're, what, ninety?
27 LOLA: Really, Constance! Ms. Peabody came highly
28   recommended.
29 POLLY: I helped a friend of Ms. Lane's out of a small
30   difficulty awhile back.
31 NORMAN: Look, unless you produce J.J., I agree with
32   Constance. You're nothing but a fraud.
33 DANIELLE: Just another parasite among so many!
34 CONSTANCE: The pot calling the kettle black!
35 POLLY: Now, please, all of you. I said I found J.J.

196

1 SYLVIA: How, Ms. Peabody? What proof do you have?
2 POLLY: For one thing, J.J. Hawkthorne did not sign
3   the rental car agreement that night.
4   *(Shocked reactions from ALL)*
5 CONSTANCE: That's ridiculous!
6 DANIELLE: The police must have checked that!
7 PHIL: Of course! And he had to show his license.
8 NORMAN: And credit card!
9 POLLY: Oh, I know at least three people I could go to
10   right now if I needed a bogus license or credit
11   card ... and, honestly, I'm ninety! Where have you
12   been?
13 LOLA: But how do you know J.J. didn't sign the
14   agreement?
15 POLLY: I checked it against J.J.'s real signature.
16 DANIELLE: Not possible! He typed everything and
17   used e-mail exclusively.
18 PHIL: That's right! I never saw a thing he wrote.
19 NORMAN: You know kids and computers.
20 SYLVIA: And even if he didn't sign the agreement,
21   where was he the night Mr. Hawkthrone died?
22 POLLY: Why, right here, of course.
23   *(BUTTLES enters Left as ALL reflect shocked*
24   *reactions.)*
25 PHIL: That's ridiculous!
26 CONSTANCE: We were the only ones here!
27 LOLA: We'll all testify to that.
28 POLLY: Of course you will, my dears.
29 NORMAN: But, Mrs. Peapod, you must have some kind
30   of proof. I mean, all this is very easy to say, but
31   hard to back up.
32 POLLY: Oh, I have proof. Right here in my knitting
33   bag.
34 BUTTLES: Ladies and gentlemen ... dinner is served.
35   *(ALL cautiously rise and move Left. POLLY leaves her*

1   *knitting bag on chair, conspicuously.)*
2 **LOLA:** *(With a laugh)* **Well, perhaps J.J. will join us for**
3   **dinner!** *(She exits Left.)*
4 **POLLY: I should hope so! I'm sure he's famished!**
5   *(POLLY exits followed by SYLVIA.)*
6 **PHIL: What do you make of this, Norman?**
7 **NORMAN: I think she's nuts.**
8 **CONSTANCE: We'd better hope so!**
9   *(PHIL, NORMAN, and CONSTANCE exit Left.*
10   *DANIELLE moves cautiously to chair as if she is about*
11   *to pick up the knitting bag. LOLA enters Left and*
12   *catches her.)*
13 **LOLA: What are you doing?**
14 **DANIELLE: Nothing! Just on my way to dinner.**
15   *(DANIELLE crosses LOLA moving Left. She pauses,*
16   *turns back glaring at LOLA.)* **Coming, Lola?**
17   *(LOLA exits Left following DANIELLE. A moment later,*
18   *PHIL backs on Right, CONSTANCE backs on nervously*
19   *Left. They bump into each other Center and scream.)*
20 **CONSTANCE: What are you doing here?**
21 **PHIL: Why, Constance! Fancy meeting you here. Are**
22   **you doing what I think you're doing?**
23 **CONSTANCE: I ... I lost my earring.**
24 **PHIL: How convenient. I see you've found it. May I**
25   **accompany you into dinner?**
26   *(PHIL offers his arm. Reluctantly CONSTANCE takes*
27   *it. They exit Left. BUTTLES enters Right carrying a*
28   *bottle of wine. He moves cautiously to the knitting bag.*
29   *NORMAN enters Left.)*
30 **NORMAN: Buttles! What's taking you so long?**
31 **BUTTLES: Coming, Mr. Newcomb. Coming.**
32   *(BUTTLES and NORMAN exit Left. A moment later*
33   *FIGURE wearing ski mask and long coat or cape enters*
34   *Right moving to knitting bag. SYLVIA enters Left. She*
35   *sees figure, who sees her.)*

1   SYLVIA: Who ... who? *(SYLVIA faints. FIGURE steals*
2   *knitting bag and exits Right as curtain falls.)*
3
4   **Scene Three**
5
6   *The Great Room, a few minutes later.*
7   *(AT RISE: SYLVIA is resting in a chair. POLLY*
8   *stands next to her, fussing. The OTHERS stand about*
9   *nervously. BUTTLES, carrying a tray holding an ice*
10   *bag, moves to POLLY.)*
11 BUTTLES: Madam, an ice bag?
12 POLLY: Thank you, Buttles. *(BUTTLES exits Right.)*
13 SYLVIA: Oh, I don't need that.
14 POLLY: Oh, my dear, I think you do. You got a nasty
15   bump when you fainted.
16   *(POLLY puts ice bag on the back of SYLVIA's head.*
17   *SYLVIA holds it there.)*
18 CONSTANCE: A bit high on the drama, wouldn't you
19   say, Sylvia?
20 NORMAN: What were you doing in here anyway?
21 SYLVIA: Well, I ... I ...
22 PHIL: Lost an earring?
23 SYLVIA: No, I just ....
24 POLLY: You wanted to look at the evidence, didn't
25   you?
26 SYLVIA: Yes. I wasn't going to take it or anything. I
27   just wanted to know.
28 DANIELLE: *(Sarcastically)* But somebody *did* steal it,
29   right?
30 NORMAN: *(Sarcastically)* Somebody wearing a cape
31   and mask.
32 LOLA: Really, Sylvia! This isn't Phantom of the Opera!
33 CONSTANCE: We all know who swiped the bag.
34 PHIL: It was you, Sylvia! You were the only one in
35   here who was alone.

1   SYLVIA: But I didn't take it!
2   LOLA: Come on! You stole it, hid it, and then pulled
3   this ridiculous fainting stunt.
4   SYLVIA: I swear I didn't! Doesn't anybody believe me?
5   POLLY: Of course I do.
6   CONSTANCE: Then who was the masked man, Ms.
7   Peapot?
8   POLLY: The same man who rented the car the night
9   Mr. Hawkthorne died.
10   LOLA: That ... that's ricidulous.
11   PHIL: Really! You'd be very good at inventing a
12   conspiracy theory.
13   POLLY: Oh, there's been a conspiracy, all right. But it's
14   not a theory. It's fact. It was very simple to have
15   someone the right age rent a car in J.J.'s name,
16   then wreck it on a bridge so it would *appear* J.J.
17   had died.
18   NORMAN: Why would anybody do such a thing?
19   POLLY: Because the young man never saw J.J.
20   Hawkthorne get off flight ninety-five from Bern.
21   CONSTANCE: What?
22   POLLY: He was watching those disembarking flight
23   ninety-five, of course, or at least as well as one can
24   when the passengers come up from customs.
25   However, when no one fitting whatever
26   description he had got off the plane, he checked
27   and found out J.J. Hawkthorne never got *on* the
28   plane! *(Shocked reactions from ALL)* So, he called his
29   accomplice, and they moved on to plan B.
30   DANIELLE: *(Clapping)* Congratulations, Ms. P. This is a
31   better plot than Tom Clancy could think up!
32   PHIL: Where do the Russian spies come in?
33   POLLY: Oh, Mr. Potts, there are no spies. This was all
34   done merely for money. The oldest motive in the
35   world.

1   SYLVIA: I don't understand, Ms. Peabody ... what was
2   plan B?
3   POLLY: The fake accident. The man who rented the
4   car opened all the windows when he got to
5   Passaquattic Bridge and ran the car over the side.
6   Empty, of course. Thus it would appear J.J. had
7   died. He left a wallet and luggage supposedly
8   belonging to J.J. in the car so it would appear J.J.
9   had died and thus could not inherit the fortune. It
10   all seemed so simple. Even the police didn't seem
11   to question the accident.
12   NORMAN: So how did the real J.J. feel about being
13   dead?
14   CONSTANCE: And not getting a penny?
15   POLLY: Safe. Very safe, for once.
16   *(BUTTLES enters Right with knitting bag on serving*
17   *tray he used for the ice bag.)*
18   PHIL: Hold on a second!
19   DANIELLE: *(Sarcastically)* Looks like the butler did it.
20   CONSTANCE: Where'd you find that thing?
21   POLLY: In the accomplice's room, Ms. Bashing.
22   SYLVIA: *(To BUTTLES)* You searched our rooms?
23   BUTTLES: On Madam's orders.
24   NORMAN: That's against the law, isn't it, Phil?
25   PHIL: I ... I don't ... well, yes, it's *got* to be!
26   POLLY: But what's important is the evidence is now
27   safe.
28   DANIELLE: What evidence?
29   POLLY: *(She pulls out papers and she mentions them.)* A
30   handwritten letter from J.J. to Mr. Hawkthorne
31   with a signature. A copy of the rental car
32   agreement with the forged signature. An affidavit
33   from the head of the Beaupres Academy attesting
34   to the identity of J.J. Hawkthorne along with a
35   picture of the child. And finally, all of your phone

1   records from the night Mr. Hawkthorne died.
2   CONSTANCE: Our phone records!
3   PHIL: How did you get them?
4   POLLY: Oh, the phone company is so nice to people
5   who are ninety years old!
6   NORMAN: You're pretty conniving, aren't you?
7   POLLY: Sometimes we have to be if we're going to find
8   the truth.
9   DANIELLE: *(Angrily)* Why did you have to hire her,
10   Lola?
11   PHIL: Looks like a very stupid thing to do!
12   LOLA: We had to know if J.J. was alive or dead!
13   POLLY: Exactly! For two reasons. First, if J.J. was
14   dead, you'd need proof so you actually could get
15   your hands on the money. Otherwise it's tied up in
16   the courts for years. Second, if J.J. was alive,
17   you'd need to locate ... and then kill her.
18   DANIELLE: Her?
19   CONSTANCE: J.J.'s a boy!
20   PHIL: He's always been a boy!
21   NORMAN: I remember seeing him when he was little.
22   He was wearing blue!
23   POLLY: Mr. Hawkthorne did indeed want to protect
24   his daughter ... from the prying eyes of the public
25   and probably from some of you. So he made
26   everybody think J.J. was a boy ... when in fact ...
27   *(She pulls a birth certificate from bag.)* her birth
28   certificate reads Jennifer Jane Hawkthorne.
29   LOLA: Well, well, well, Ms. Peabody ... you've certainly
30   done your job well. I wish, however, you'd have
31   given me this information in private.
32   POLLY: *(Sweetly)* Oh, my dear, I wouldn't have wanted
33   to give you anything in private. You probably
34   would have killed me and poor Jennifer as well!
35   LOLA: Me? Why ... what are you talking about?

1 POLLY: Buttles, in which room did you find the bag?
2 BUTTLES: Ms. Lane's room, Madam.
3 LOLA: That's a lie!
4 BUTTLES: *(Indignantly)* I beg your pardon! *(BUTTLES*
5 *exits Left.)*
6 LOLA: Then ... then somebody put it there to frame
7 me!
8 POLLY: I'm afraid not. Yours was the only phone to
9 receive a call from JFK a year ago tonight ... the
10 night J.J. supposedly died.
11 LOLA: Well, I ... I had other friends coming in that
12 night.
13 POLLY: More importantly, you're next in line to
14 inherit. If you could prove J.J. was dead, which
15 you and your partner intended, then you would
16 have been a very, very rich woman. You thought I
17 might be able to come up with J.J.'s whereabouts,
18 and I have.
19 LOLA: Archie! Archie!
20 *(FIGURE, now minus the mask and cape, enters Right.*
21 *It's ARCHIE ADAMS, a tough looking character. He*
22 *carries a small canister.)*
23 ARCHIE: You got trouble, Lola?
24 LOLA: Just a little.
25 SYLVIA: You! You're the one who stole the bag!
26 ARCHIE: I didn't steal nothin'. I'll deny it all the way
27 to the Supreme Court.
28 POLLY: Just as you'll deny renting the car and driving
29 it into the river.
30 ARCHIE: I don't know nothin' about nothin'!
31 LOLA: *(Coyly)* Except how to get rid of evidence.
32 ARCHIE: Yeah! See this? *(ARCHIE holds up canister.)*
33 LOLA: Sonamulate X.
34 POLLY: A sleeping gas!
35 ARCHIE: Yeah ... it'll send you all into a nice snooze.

1   LOLA: Unfortunately you won't wake up.

2   ARCHIE: 'Cause I got some matches here, see —

3   *(BUTTLES enters Right behind ARCHIE.)*

4   LOLA: They don't need the details, Archie! Just pull

5   the plug!

6   *(BUTTLES knocks ARCHIE out with a frying pan or*

7   *wine bottle. ARCHIE falls to the floor, the canister*

8   *rolling wherever. NORMAN picks it up gingerly.)*

9   LOLA: Why, you! *(LOLA turns to run Off Left, but PHIL*

10   *and CONSTANCE stop her.)*

11   POLLY: Oh, thank goodness, Buttles!

12   SYLVIA: What would we have done without you?

13   BUTTLES: I will always watch out for you, Ms.

14   Hawkthorne.

15   PHIL: You're J.J.?

16   SYLVIA: Yes, Mr. Potts. The real J.J.

17   LOLA: But you were here long before that night!

18   SYLVIA: Of course. Father e-mailed me about his

19   failing health, and I came directly home. But he

20   suspected someone would try something, so he

21   hired me as his secretary just to keep me safe. His

22   last words to me were "Be careful."

23   POLLY: Jennifer knew one of you would eventually

24   make a move.

25   LOLA: I had to know where J.J. was! Can't you see

26   that? I had to know!

27   POLLY: My dear, she was right under your nose!

28   *(The curtain falls.)*

Where Did Everybody Go?

Synopsis:
Sunken treasure has lured explorers since the beginning of time. But when an expedition from the Sea Hawk comes upon what appears to be an abandoned ocean liner shrouded in fog, they find more than they bargained for.

Characters (1 male, 3 female):
ERIC MADDOX, sea salvage company owner
REBECCA HARRIS, archaeologist
WENDY HUNT, shareholder in the expedition
PAMELA, woman on the ship

Setting:
The lounge on a small liner which once sailed the Mediterranean Sea filled with tourists. We see a few cafe tables still set with plates of food and half-filled drink glasses along with chairs, some of which are overturned. A closed door Up Center, a desk Left, scattered with papers. A life preserver hangs on Upstage wall on one side of the door. An activity chalkboard hangs askew on the other side, a few words still visible: shuffleboard, tango lessons, table tennis. A few times for these activities are also shown on the chalkboard. Dust covers everything providing a haunting vision.

Props:
Metal box or suitcase (radio); backpack; piece of very stale bread; new notebook; headphones for radio; telegram; book; dog leash; old log book or journal; wooden box beautifully decorated in gold with Greek figures; fire ax; chain with wrist band attached; water bottle; working flashlight; old, worn notebook.

Costumes:
Eric, Rebecca, and Wendy dress in modern clothes, wearing T-shirts and shorts, whatever one might wear on an open boat in hot weather. Pamela is dressed in a white floor-length gown. Her hair is done up in a forties fashion. While she is generally very pale, her lips are ruby red.

Sound Effect:
Banging pipes, as indicated. Use a hammer on a length of metal pipe.

1   **Scene One**
2
3   *(AT RISE: the stage is empty. A moment passes.)*
4   **ERIC:** *(Calling from Off Left)* **Ahoy! Anyone aboard?**
5   *(ERIC enters Left, carrying a metal box.)* **Hello?**
6   **Anyone here?**
7   *(WENDY enters Left as ERIC sets metal box on table.)*
8   **WENDY: What's going on?**
9   **ERIC: Your guess is as good as mine.**
10   **WENDY: Look at this place!** *(REBECCA enters Left*
11   *carrying a backpack holding water, a book or two, and*
12   *various papers. WENDY moves to cafe table set with*
13   *food.)* **At least they've got lunch ready for us.**
14   *(WENDY picks up a piece of bread which crumbles to*
15   *dust.)*
16   **REBECCA: We should have eaten before we left**
17   **Santorini this morning.**
18   **ERIC: Let's not start grumbling about that now. You**
19   **were the one who wanted to get an early start,**
20   **Rebecca.**
21   **REBECCA: I know, I know. I just had this feeling that**
22   **today would be our lucky day.**
23   **WENDY:** *(With a laugh)* **If you call this lucky.**
24   **REBECCA: We don't even know exactly what it is!**
25   **ERIC: A liner of some type.**
26   **WENDY:** *(Looking at the activity board)* **Carried at least**
27   **a few fun-loving passengers. Look here,**
28   **shuffleboard ... table tennis ... tango lessons.**
29   **REBECCA: Tango lessons? That's out of another era.**
30   **WENDY: Oh, come on!** *(WENDY grabs ERIC and begins a*
31   *quick tango, humming as they both dance, he*
32   *reluctantly.)*
33   **ERIC:** *(After a few steps)* **All right, Wendy! All right!**
34   **WENDY: What a stuffed shirt! I'm paying for this**
35   **expedition.**

1   ERIC: We have other investors, you know.
2   WENDY: Then you can tango with them when you get
3   back to Barcelona.
4   ERIC: *(Looking around the room sadly)* I don't really feel
5   like tangoing at all.
6   REBECCA: Yeah, this place *is* kind of creepy.
7   WENDY: To an archaeologist? Oh, Rebecca, get serious.
8   I'd think this would be the Holy Grail to someone
9   like you.
10   REBECCA: It's got its moments ... but there's
11   something ... I don't know.
12   ERIC: What was the temperature before we moved into
13   that fog?
14   REBECCA: *(Checking a notebook)* Just a second.
15   WENDY: It was hot! I can tell you that without
16   checking notes.
17   REBECCA: For the sake of accuracy it was twenty-
18   eight degrees centigrade.
19   ERIC: *(Whistling)* Hot enough to fry an egg on deck ...
20   but in here it's pretty cold and clammy.
21   WENDY: A bit more of a tango and we could heat
22   things up.
23   REBECCA: What do you think, Eric?
24   ERIC: This ship must hold a couple of hundred
25   passengers.
26   WENDY: Where are they, then?
27   REBECCA: It doesn't look like anyone's been on board
28   for years.
29   WENDY: *(Pointing to food on tables)* So explain lunch.
30   ERIC: Could it have broken away from its moorings
31   during a storm and just drifted?
32   REBECCA: Someone would have seen it. Somehow.
33   The Mediterranean is big, but ships are passing
34   each other all the time.
35   ERIC: Look ... we've got to search this thing. There

1   could be someone, somewhere in trouble. Wendy
2   and I'll search, and Rebecca, I've got our portable
3   radio here. See if you can reach someone and call
4   for help.
5   WENDY: Oh, Eric, we're wasting time on this thing.
6   Let's go back to the *Sea Hawk* and get back on
7   track. Our expedition is to find the wreck of the
8   *Poseidon*, not some old fossil.
9   REBECCA: Doesn't this intrigue you?
10   WENDY: The amphora full of gold on the *Poseidon*
11   intrigues me. The point is to get my investment
12   back, not to catch some horrible disease on this
13   old hulk.
14   ERIC: All right ... all right. We're not far from where
15   the *Poseidon* is supposed to have gone down. Let's
16   give this an hour. We'll search the ship. Rebecca,
17   you see if you can reach the Greek authorities and
18   alert them there's a ship out here ... and then we'll
19   give it up.
20   WENDY: One hour.
21   ERIC: Shouldn't even take that long to look through
22   this thing.
23   *(REBECCA places metal case on table and opens the*
24   *top. She pulls out headphones and, still standing,*
25   *adjusts buttons, etc., all of which the audience can't see*
26   *because top of the case blocks their view.)*
27   WENDY: Which way, Captain?
28   ERIC: How about tackling the port side.
29   WENDY: I love sailor talk!
30   *(ERIC leads WENDY Off Right.)*
31   REBECCA: *(Into headphones)* *Sea Hawk* to anyone. *Sea*
32   *Hawk* to anyone. Come in! Come in! *(We hear very*
33   *faint crying Offstage. REBECCA takes off the*
34   *headphones.)* Hello? Anyone here? *(She shrugs, puts*
35   *the headphones on, turns the power on, but gets*

1   *nothing. She plays with the buttons, frustrated.)* **Sea**

2   ***Hawk*** **to anyone! Come in anyone! Come in!**

3   *(The curtain falls.)*

4

5   **Scene Two**

6

7   *The same, forty-five minutes later.*

8   *(AT RISE: The stage is empty. ERIC and WENDY enter*

9   *Left.)*

10 **ERIC: Rebecca? It's a total wash.**

11 **WENDY: No one —** *(They notice REBECCA is gone.)*

12   **Nothing.**

13 **ERIC:** *(Looking around the room, worried)* **Rebecca!**

14 **WENDY: Rebecca!**

15 **ERIC: What do you think ...**

16 **WENDY: I think we should get off this thing.**

17 **ERIC: Rebecca!**

18 **WENDY: The radio's still here.**

19   *(ERIC flips it on.)*

20 **ERIC: Funny. No power. Nothing.**

21 **WENDY: Well, we would have seen her wandering**

22   **around, wouldn't we?**

23 **ERIC: Or at least heard her.**

24 **WENDY: This ship's still as death!**

25 **ERIC: Rebecca!**

26 **WENDY: Look, I don't know what's going on, so let's go**

27   **back to the *Sea Hawk*.**

28 **ERIC: We can't leave without Rebecca.**

29 **WENDY: I mean then we can radio for help or**

30   **something. This little thing** *(Indicating radio)* **is**

31   **probably too small to pick up anything.**

32 **ERIC: It's got a radius of five hundred miles. Even if**

33   **the batteries are weak.**

34 **WENDY: But apparently, they're dead.**

35   *(REBECCA enters Left.)*

1 REBECCA: And so's the radio on the *Sea Hawk*.
2 ERIC: Rebecca! Where have you been?
3 REBECCA: I couldn't get this thing to work, so I went
4   back to the *Sea Hawk*.
5 ERIC: That wasn't smart.
6 REBECCA: Eric, I'm a big girl. It's tethered right next
7   to the gangway, so don't worry. I didn't fall in, and
8   there aren't any sharks around.
9 ERIC: I know, but —
10 WENDY: Let me get this straight, Rebecca, the radio
11   on the *Sea Hawk* doesn't work either?
12 REBECCA: Couldn't get a thing.
13 WENDY: That doesn't make a lot of sense. You've got
14   good equipment, Eric!
15 ERIC: Sunken Glory Expeditions has the *best*
16   equipment!
17 WENDY: So what's wrong with it?
18 ERIC: It's got to be something with the weather.
19   Maybe the fog's causing interference or something.
20 WENDY: Let's just get out of here and go find the
21   *Poseidon*. Your investors will appreciate it.
22 ERIC: You're right.
23 REBECCA: *(Moving to desk)* But aren't you curious
24   about this ship? I mean ... we don't even know its
25   name.
26 WENDY: It's covered in rust. That's all we need to
27   know.
28 REBECCA: Look at this ... the calendar is for 1946.
29 ERIC: 1946?
30 REBECCA: And here's a telegram ... it's dated October
31   twenty-first, 1946.
32 WENDY: This is really creeping me out!
33 ERIC: What's the telegram say?
34 REBECCA: It's a bit faded. *(Reading)* "Professor
35   Reimer, Congratulations on your astounding find.

1   Will wait for you in Harwich. My mouth is sealed.
2   Signed A.R." *(Thinking)* Reimer ... Reimer ...
3 ERIC: Ring any bells?
4   *(REBECCA pulls book from backpack.)*
5 WENDY: Rebecca, this isn't our quest. Our quest is out
6   there on the *Sea Hawk* looking for the *Poseidon.*
7   There's treasure to be found there. I ... I don't get
8   the feeling ... there's much treasure on board this
9   thing.
10 REBECCA: But what would Reimer have found?
11 WENDY: For all we know he was a private detective
12   looking for a long, lost poodle.
13 REBECCA: *(Finding a page in the book)* No ... no ...
14   Reimer wasn't a poodle hunter. He was an
15   archaeologist. I knew his name sounded familiar.
16 ERIC: Must have been famous. He's in your book.
17 REBECCA: He was one of the first to authenticate the
18   location of the ancient city of Troy ... he excavated
19   parts of Pompeii, and then worked on the city of
20   Persepolis. He disappeared in 1946 while on board
21   the *S.S. Suez,* a liner that disappeared and was
22   presumably sunk during a violent storm.
23 ERIC: Whoa! Can this be the *Suez?*
24 WENDY: I'm out of here! *(WENDY moves Left.)*
25 REBECCA: But Reimer must have found something
26   very valuable. Very important ...
27 ERIC: Like what?
28 REBECCA: I don't know ... but it's somewhere on this
29   ship.
30   *(We hear a knocking, as a hammer on a pipe.)*
31 WENDY: And that is what?
32 ERIC: Sounds like ... plumbing.
33 WENDY: Eric, there's no one on this ship who needs to
34   use the plumbing!
35 REBECCA: Are you sure you looked everywhere?

1   ERIC: In every closet, corner, and cabinet.
2   REBECCA: You mean everything was unlocked?
3   WENDY: Strange, but true.
4   *(The knocking stops.)*
5   REBECCA: Did you go through the ship's hold?
6   ERIC: Yeah ... we didn't open every crate, but called
7   out.
8   WENDY: And if they couldn't hear us they were either
9   very deaf or very dead.
10   ERIC: And if this ship was last seen in 1946, I'd vote
11   for the latter.
12   WENDY: Look, there couldn't be anybody on this ship.
13   Let's just get off ourselves.
14   REBECCA: But Professor Reimer's discovery. It must
15   still be on this ship. You must have looked in his
16   room.
17   ERIC: Now how would we have known his room?
18   REBECCA: Did you find a room with charts,
19   drawings? Any amorphae?
20   WENDY: There was one ... three doors down on the
21   starboard side.
22   ERIC: A couple of jugs were lying in the corner.
23   *(REBECCA races Off Left.)*
24   WENDY: Look Eric ...
25   *(ERIC is looking around the room. He picks up a dog*
26   *leash.)*
27   ERIC: Look. I wonder what happened to the dog.
28   WENDY: You two need to stop your wondering.
29   Curiosity killed the cat!
30   ERIC: But it also finds millions and millions in sunken
31   treasure.
32   WENDY: That's right. And that's what we're supposed
33   to be looking for.
34   *(ERIC pulls book from his pocket.)*
35   ERIC: I forgot I'd taken this from the bridge.

1   WENDY: What is it?
2   ERIC: Looks like the navigator's log. *(ERIC flips to the*
3   *last page and reads.)* "Thick fog. Instruments
4   contradictory. Captain says stay course. Incessant
5   banging of pipes, but calm seas. Passengers
6   anxious."
7   WENDY: Well?
8   ERIC: That's it. So where did everybody go?
9   WENDY: Maybe they got in the lifeboats and got away.
10   ERIC: Every lifeboat is still in place. We checked every
11   one, remember?
12   *(REBECCA enters carrying a box with an open lid.)*
13   REBECCA: Did you see this?
14   ERIC: Just lying on the floor, right?
15   WENDY: Turned over.
16   REBECCA: Yeah.
17   ERIC: Didn't look very important.
18   REBECCA: It's beautiful, though. *(REBECCA dusts it*
19   *off.)* Look at the figures and design.
20   WENDY: Then let's take it and go.
21   REBECCA: Odd, because they didn't make a lot of
22   boxes back then for carrying things.
23   ERIC: When's "Back then"?
24   REBECCA: This could be as old as one thousand B.C.
25   WENDY: With those hinges? I doubt that, kiddo.
26   REBECCA: Maybe you're right.
27   *(We hear a faint crying Offstage.)*
28   WENDY: Shhh! Do you hear something?
29   ERIC: No.
30   REBECCA: I do. Someone's crying.
31   WENDY: But that's ridiculous.
32   *(The crying becomes louder.)*
33   ERIC: Someone's crying! Someone's on this ship!
34   REBECCA: Hello? Hello?
35   PAMELA: *(From Off Center, weakly)* Help me!

1   WENDY: What's that?

2   PAMELA: *(From Off Center)* Let me out!

3   ERIC: Hello? Where are you? Where are you?

4   REBECCA: We can help you!

5   PAMELA: *(From Off Center)* I don't know.

6   ERIC: Keep talking. We'll find you!

7   PAMELA: *(From Off Center)* Help! Let me out! Let me

8   out!

9   WENDY: Eric ... *(Indicating door at Center)* we didn't

10   look in here! *(WENDY taps on the door Center.)* Hello?

11   Are you in here?

12   PAMELA: *(From Off Center)* Let me out! Please, let me

13   out!

14   ERIC: *(Trying to open the door)* It's stuck.

15   REBECCA: It's locked!

16   ERIC: We need to find something ...

17   PAMELA: *(From Off Center)* Help! Let me out! Let me

18   out!

19   WENDY: We've got to hurry! She could be dying!

20   REBECCA: Eric ... just outside there's an ax in the fire

21   box.

22   *(ERIC exits Left.)*

23   WENDY: We're finding something to open the door.

24   PAMELA: *(From Off Center)* Please ... let me out.

25   WENDY: It won't be but a moment!

26   *(ERIC returns with ax. He uses the blade to pry open*

27   *the door.)*

28   REBECCA: We've got something to open the door with!

29   WENDY: Hurry, Eric!

30   ERIC: How can somebody be inside there?

31   REBECCA: We don't know, but there is somebody!

32   PAMELA: *(From Off Center)* Hurry, please! Hurry ...

33   ERIC: I've almost got it open.

34   REBECCA: Hang on! We're coming!

35   ERIC: There!

1   *(He hands the ax to WENDY, and then pries the door*
2   *open. PAMELA stands at Center. A metal band around*
3   *her left wrist is connected to a chain that is hooked*
4   *somewhere in the room. She has enough chain to move*
5   *to Center Stage.)*
6   **PAMELA: Thanks ever so much. I thought I'd be in**
7   **there forever.** *(ERIC, REBECCA, and WENDY are too*
8   *stunned to speak.)* **My name's Pamela.**
9   **ERIC:** *(Weakly)* **I'm Eric. Eric Maddox.** *(Indicating*
10   *REBECCA and WENDY)* **Rebecca Harris ... and**
11   **Wendy Hunt.**
12   **PAMELA: Ever so pleased to meet you.**
13   **WENDY: What were you doing in there?**
14   **PAMELA: I'm afraid I was a naughty girl.** *(PAMELA*
15   *holds up her wrist, showing them the chain.)*
16   **ERIC: What is going on?**
17   **PAMELA: I haven't the foggiest! But I certainly could**
18   **use a drink.**
19   *(REBECCA moves to the things she brought on the ship.*
20   *She pulls a water bottle out.)*
21   **REBECCA: Here. It's warm, but it's wet.**
22   **PAMELA: How quaint! Water.** *(PAMELA takes a sip.)*
23   **Better. Much better.**
24   **ERIC: Look ... this doesn't make any sense.**
25   **PAMELA: I only took the cigarette case because of the**
26   **diamonds, but Mrs. Godfrey made such a fuss the**
27   **captain had to make a show of me. Honestly! The**
28   **old bat could have easily bought ten more without**
29   **blinking an eye.** *(No response)* **Where ... where is**
30   **everyone?** *(PAMELA looks around the room.)* **It's a**
31   **terrible mess, isn't it? What happened?**
32   **REBECCA: Pamela, what year is it?**
33   **PAMELA:** *(With a laugh)* **1946, of course!**
34   **WENDY: Oh, boy! Oh, boy! We should have gotten off**
35   **when we had the chance!**

1   PAMELA: What's wrong? It's 1946 ... although you
2   certainly aren't dressed for first class.
3   REBECCA: It's not 1946, Pamela. It's 2006. *(Or current*
4   *year)*
5   PAMELA: Look who's pulling whose leg now!
6   ERIC: Look, Pamela, something really strange has
7   happened here. There's no way to explain it, but
8   Rebecca's right. It's 2006, and I think we're the
9   first people to board this ship since 1946.
10   PAMELA: That's ... that's ... insane!
11   WENDY: What was the name of the ship you boarded?
12   PAMELA: The *Suez. S.S.Suez.*
13   REBECCA: Where did you leave from?
14   PAMELA: Beirut, bound for Harwich. I'm going home
15   to visit my family.
16   ERIC: Something happened ... a fog seems to have
17   overtaken the ship.
18   PAMELA: Is that so odd? Oh, that strange professor
19   kept shouting about something horrible happening
20   and that somebody had been through his stuff, but
21   ... we all thought he was just joking.
22   WENDY: *(Searching through backpack)* Maybe we ought
23   to try and get that chain off.
24   PAMELA: Would you? It's so humiliating!
25   WENDY: I'll see what it's hooked to. *(WENDY pulls out*
26   *a flashlight and turns it on. Cautiously she enters room*
27   *where PAMELA was kept.)*
28   REBECCA: Was it Professor Reimer who was
29   shouting?
30   PAMELA: Yes! Where is he? That old fool's probably
31   behind all this!
32   ERIC: There's no one on the ship, Pamela. Not a single
33   person. *(WENDY screams from inside the room, then*
34   *enters Center.)* What's wrong?
35   WENDY: Oh, no ... no ... *(WENDY sits on chair as ERIC*

1   *takes flashlight and exits Center into room.)*
2   REBECCA: *(To PAMELA)* What's in there?
3   PAMELA: I ... I don't know! There was no light! I
4   spent all night in the dark.
5   REBECCA: All night? It's been sixty years!
6   *(ERIC enters Center.)*
7   ERIC: Who is that, Pamela?
8   PAMELA: Who's who?
9   WENDY: The skeleton! There's a skeleton lying on the
10   floor in there!
11   PAMELA: Oh! Oh, no! I ... I never knew that! It was
12   dark! It was dark all night ... and *(The banging of*
13   *the pipes starts again. It is rhythmic and haunting.)*
14   Stop it! Stop it! All night we heard that terrible
15   noise! All night!
16   REBECCA: Pamela, did Professor Reimer tell anyone
17   about what he found on his expedition?
18   PAMELA: I never talked to him! Most of the
19   passengers didn't think he was very friendly ...
20   *(REBECCA exits Left.)*
21   ERIC: Rebecca! Where are you going? Rebecca?
22   PAMELA: *(Indicating chain)* Oh, please, can you help
23   me get rid of this thing?
24   WENDY: How could someone just rot away in there?
25   PAMELA: I'm afraid it's very tight around my wrist.
26   ERIC: What's the end of this hooked to, Wendy?
27   WENDY: It's soldered into a wall rivet.
28   ERIC: That's not good.
29   PAMELA: Perhaps your ax would help.
30   ERIC: Worth a try. *(ERIC pulls chain so it is visible to the*
31   *audience. He places it flat on the floor. This allows*
32   *PAMELA to stand while he is working. ERIC takes the*
33   *ax and begins hitting the chain with little success.)* The
34   chain's tempered steel.
35   PAMELA: Is that bad?

1 ERIC: Almost impossible to break through.
2 WENDY: Is there anything on the *Sea Hawk* that might
3   help, Eric?
4 ERIC: If this doesn't work, I've got a couple of other
5   things that I can try.
6 PAMELA: Do hurry. It's so inconvenient. *(The banging*
7   *stops as REBECCA enters Left carrying a notebook.)*
8   Oh, that awful sound! I hope I never hear it again!
9 REBECCA: *(Frightened)* Eric?
10   *(ERIC stops his work and moves to REBECCA.)*
11 ERIC: What's that?
12 REBECCA: A notebook from Professor Reimer's cabin.
13 WENDY: I wish I'd never heard that name!
14 ERIC: What's it say?
15 REBECCA: Just words. Random words ... *Suez* ...
16 WENDY: The name of this tub.
17 REBECCA: *Poseidon* ...
18 WENDY: What? We've been looking for the *Poseidon*!
19   *(ERIC returns to his work, hitting the chain with the*
20   *ax.)*
21 REBECCA: Hades ...
22 WENDY: That's appropriate.
23 REBECCA: Epimetheus.
24 WENDY: Epimetheus?
25 REBECCA: Prometheus.
26 WENDY: Who stole fire from the gods and gave it to
27   the world.
28 REBECCA: Epimetheus was his brother.
29 PAMELA: I didn't know you still cared about such
30   things!
31 REBECCA: What do they have to do with you, Pamela?
32 PAMELA: Oh, Rebecca, absolutely nothing. How are
33   you coming down there, Eric?
34 ERIC: It's chipping ... chipping away.
35 REBECCA: Eric ... wait!

1   *(ERIC stops his work.)*
2 PAMELA: No, darling, keep working! It seems to be
3   getting tighter. My wrist hurts terribly.
4 REBECCA: What is *Suez* spelled backwards?
5 WENDY: Zeus.
6 ERIC: Zeus ... the greatest of all immortals.
7 PAMELA: Eric, darling, please! I'm getting impatient!
8 REBECCA: Zeus who wanted to punish mankind for
9   accepting Prometheus's gift of fire.
10   *(ERIC has returned to work.)*
11 PAMELA: Oh, hurry, Eric!
12 REBECCA: Zeus had Hephaestos make a woman in his
13   forge ... a woman he gave to Prometheus's brother
14   Epimetheus.
15 PAMELA: You certainly know your mythology,
16   Rebecca, darling.
17 ERIC: So where's this going, Rebecca?
18 REBECCA: She was very intelligent, but very curious!
19 WENDY: Like someone else I know!
20 REBECCA: And one day ... *(REBECCA picks up the box.)*
21 PAMELA: Where did you get that thing?
22 REBECCA: Professor Reimer found it. Epimetheus was
23   warned not to accept anything from Zeus. He was
24   warned, but the woman failed to heed the
25   warning.
26 PAMELA: It's such a beautiful box, isn't it?
27 ERIC: Hey! The steel's more brittle than I thought! I
28   can get through this with a few more whacks.
29 REBECCA: Eric! The woman took the box from a
30   stranger who told her not to look inside. Under no
31   circumstances was she to look inside!
32 ERIC: But curiosity killed the cat!
33 PAMELA: A few more whacks, Eric! Now hurry,
34   please!
35 WENDY: She opened the box!

1 REBECCA: Her name was Pandora!
2 WENDY: Oh, Rebecca, that ... that can't be!
3 REBECCA: Stop, Eric! Stop!
4 *(ERIC stops in mid-swing.)*
5 PAMELA: Eric, you can't leave me like this!
6 REBECCA: All the evils of the world came rushing out
7 of the box!
8 WENDY: This box ...
9 ERIC: And it's open.
10 PAMELA: You don't believe this nonsense! Eric,
11 please! I've been in there forever!
12 REBECCA: Professor Reimer's skeleton lies on the
13 floor in there.
14 PAMELA: *(Blithely)* Really, I don't know anything
15 about a skeleton!
16 WENDY: And what happened to everyone else?
17 REBECCA: Disease, pestilence, hopelessness ... war ...
18 world war! You ... you were forced into the box,
19 and that ended the war, didn't it? You were locked
20 away for only a short time until someone on this
21 ship opened Pandora's box once again!
22 PAMELA: *(Laughing nastily)* You're crazy! You're all
23 crazy!
24 *(ERIC exits Center.)*
25 WENDY: What can we do, Rebecca?
26 REBECCA: I ... I don't know ...
27 PAMELA: Eric! What are you doing? *(The chain becomes*
28 *taut. The banging pipes are heard and increase in*
29 *volume and rhythm under last dialog.)* Eric, stop it!
30 ERIC: Help me, Rebecca! Help me!
31 PAMELA: You know you can't harm me! *(REBECCA*
32 *and WENDY begin to push PAMELA Off Up Center as*
33 *the pipes continue to bang.)* Nothing can harm me!
34 REBECCA: But you're harmless at sea! As long as the
35 *Suez* never docks ...

1   **PAMELA:** *(Laughing viciously)* **Oh, my dears, you think**

2   **there isn't evil in the world? Just look around!**

3   **Just look around!**

4   **WENDY: But there will be a little less now!**

5   *(REBECCA and WENDY push PAMELA Off Up*

6   *Center. The door slams shut behind them, leaving the*

7   *stage empty and silent. A beat, then)*

8   **PAMELA:** *(From Off Center)* **Let me out! You'll let me**

9   **out, won't you? Please?**

10   *(The curtain falls.)*

About the Author

Chicago-born playwright Craig Sodaro began writing plays in grade school and continued creating unusual dramatic pieces (such as *The Dismembered Pencil*) in high school. While attending Marquette University in Milwaukee, he studied playwriting and had several shows produced by the university theatre company, the Marquette Players. With a degree in journalism and English, Sodaro began a teaching career that would last thirty-three years. During that time he continued to write plays, often for schools or theatrical groups with which he worked. This led to his first published play, *Forlorn at the Fort* in *Plays* magazine, a melodrama written for the Wyoming-based Frontier Outlaw Troupe which he directed for thirteen years. In 1976 his first full-length play, *Tea and Arsenic*, appeared, and since that time he has had over one hundred plays published by various play publishers. His plays *Hush, Little Baby* and *Second Hand Kid* were performed in New York and Los Angeles, and his works have been produced around the world. Eight of his plays have recently been translated into Dutch. Sodaro now writes full time and lives high in the Colorado Rockies with his wife Sue.

Order Form

Meriwether Publishing Ltd.
PO Box 7710
Colorado Springs CO 80933-7710
Phone: 800-937-5297   Fax: 719-594-9916
Website: www.meriwether.com

Please send me the following books:

_____ **Make It Mystery #BK-B287**   **$19.95**
by Craig Sodaro
An anthology of short mystery plays

_____ **On Stage! Short Plays for Acting Students**   **$16.95**
#BK-B165
by Robert Mauro
24 short one-act plays for acting practice

_____ **Two Character Plays for Student Actors**   **$16.95**
#BK-B174
by Robert Mauro
A collection of 15 one-act plays

_____ **100 Great Monologs #BK-B276**   **$15.95**
by Rebecca Young
A collection of monologs, duologs and triologs for actors

_____ **Scenes Keep Happening #BK-B280**   **$15.95**
by Mary Krell-Oishi
More real-life snapshots of teen lives

_____ **Theatre Games for Young Performers**   **$16.95**
#BK-B188
by Maria C. Novelly
Improvisations and exercises for developing acting skills

_____ **112 Acting Games #BK-B277**   **$17.95**
by Gavin Levy
A comprehensive workbook of theatre games

These and other fine Meriwether Publishing books are available at
your local bookstore or direct from the publisher. Prices subject to
change without notice. Check our website or call for current prices.

Name: _____ e-mail: _____

Organization name: _____

Address: _____

City: _____ State: _____

Zip: _____ Phone: _____

❏ **Check enclosed**

❏ **Visa / MasterCard / Discover #** _____

                                        Expiration
Signature: _____ date: _____
        (required for credit card orders)

Colorado residents: Please add 3% sales tax.
Shipping: Include $3.95 for the first book and 75¢ for each additional book ordered.

❏ *Please send me a copy of your complete catalog of books and plays.*